LESS STRESS
MORE SUCCESS

ENGLISH REVISION FOR JUNIOR CERTIFICATE
HIGHER LEVEL

Larry Cotter

GILL & MACMILLAN

Gill & Macmillan Ltd
Hume Avenue
Park West
Dublin 12
with associated companies throughout the world
www.gillmacmillan.ie

978 0 7171 4168 5

Print origination in Ireland by O'K Graphic Design, Dublin

The paper used in this book is made from the wood pulp of managed forests. For every tree felled, at least one tree is planted, thereby renewing natural resources.

Contents

Acknowledgments

For permission to reproduce copyright material, grateful acknowledgment is made to the following:

Tim Dowling for the article 'Darling, Don't Do That'; *The Irish Times* for an extract from the article 'A Swim for the Soul' by Róisín Ingle and for the article 'Shhhhhhhhhh!' (in edited form) by Hugh Linehan; by kind permission from RTÉ, Catherine Ann Cullen for the essay 'From Bedtime Tales' and Anthony Glavin for the extract from 'In Praise of Goldfish' (in edited form); 'What There Is to See At the Zoo', © 1955 by Marianne Moore, renewed, from *The Complete Prose Of Marianne Moore* by Marianne Moore, edited by Patricia C. Willis. Used by permission of Viking Penguin, a division of Penguin Group (USA) Inc.; *In Patagonia* by Bruce Chatwin, published by Jonathan Cape. Reprinted by permission of The Random House Group Ltd; New Island Books for the extracts from *The Secret Life of the Irish Male* by Joe O'Connor and *Paul Durcan's Diary* by Paul Durcan; extract from *Pictures in my Head* by Gabriel Byrne (Wolfhound Press, 1999) reproduced by permission of Wolfhound Press, Dublin. © Gabriel Byrne 1994, 1999; Frances Cotter for the extract from the short story 'Snot's Green Sea'; Rebecca Smyth for the composition 'My Pet Hates'; Marcella McGahon for the extract from the diary *Marcella McGahon's Diary*; David Higham Associates for the extract from *Out of the Ashes* by Michael Morpurgo, published by Macmillan Children's Books; T.F. MacGahon for his letter; by permission of Penguin Books Ltd, approximately 243 words from *Adrian Mole And The Weapons Of Mass Destruction* by Sue Townsend (Michael Joseph, 2004), text © Sue Townsend, 2004, approximately 685 words from *Stone Cold* by Robert Swindells (Hamish Hamilton, 1993), © Robert Swindells, 1993; © Joanna Douglas/ Uncut/IPC+Syndication for the film review 'Bear Naked'; *The Irish Independent* for the book review 'At last, a Rival for J.K. and Harry' by Mary Shine Thompson and the article 'Want to be Cool? Tune into TG4' by Samantha McCaughran; *The Irish Daily Mail* for the article 'Golden Girl Derval is in a world of her own' by Shane McGrath; *Amphibians* first published in 1992 by Josef Weinberger Ltd (pka Warner/Chappell Plays Ltd) © 1992 by Billy Roche. Reprinted by permission of Josef Weinberger Ltd. Applications for performances (including staged readings) should be addressed to Josef Weinberger Plays Ltd, 12-14 Mortimer Street, London, W1T 3JJ; the extract from *Boat Memory* by Laline Paull is reproduced by permission of The Agency (London) Ltd © Laline Paull. All rights reserved and enquiries to The Agency (London) Ltd, 24 Pottery Lane, London, W11 4LZ, info@theagency.co.uk; 'In Memory of George Best' by Dermot Bolger, © Dermot Bolger (2005), reproduced by permission of the author; 'Born Yesterday' and 'Coming' by Philip Larkin are reprinted from *The Less Deceived* by permission of The Marvell Press, England and Australia; 'Fireworks' by James Reeves, © James Reeves from *Complete Poems For Children* (Heinemann) and reprinted by permission of the James Reeves Estate; Carcanet Press Ltd for the poem 'Miracle on St David's Day' by Gillian Clarke from *Letter from a Far Country*, 1982; 'Carentan O Carentan' by Louis Simpson from *A Dream of Governors* (Wesleyan University Press, 1959), © 1959 by Louis Simpson and reprinted by permission of Wesleyan University Press; 'Watching Walls' by Mary O'Gorman, © Mary O'Gorman; 'Leaning into the afternoons ...' from *Selected Poems* by Pablo Neruda, translated and edited by Nathaniel Tarn and published by Jonathan Cape and reprinted by permission of The Random House Group Ltd; 'My Room' by Patrick Kavanagh is reprinted from *Collected Poems*, edited by Antointette Quinn (Allen Lane, 2004), by kind permission of the Trustees of the Estate of the late Katherine B. Kavanagh, through the Jonathan Williams Literary Agency; 'The Dragon Ring of Connla', © Estate of Patricia Lynch, reprinted by kind permission of Mercier Press Ltd, Cork; 'The Ring' by Bryan MacMahon, by permission of A. P. Watt Ltd on behalf of Maurice F. MacMahon; extract from *Circle of Friends* by Maeve Binchy, published by Century/Arrow, reprinted by permission of The Random House Group Ltd; Doubleday Broadway Publishing Group for the short story 'August 2025: There will come soft rains' by Ray Bradbury from *The Martian Chronicles*; Text © 2001 Anthony Horowitz from *Point Blanc* by Anthony Horowitz, reproduced by permission of Walker Books Ltd, London, SE11 5HJ; Mark Roper for the poem 'Van Gogh's Yellow Chair'. The full version of 'Van Gogh's Yellow Chair' appears in *Something Beginning With P*, edited by Seamus Cashman, The O'Brien Press, 2004.

For permission to reproduce photographs, the author and publisher gratefully acknowledge the following:
69 © Action Images Ltd; 2, 54, 107, 128, 164 © Alamy Images; 118 Courtesy of the Council, National Army Museum, London, UK/The Bridgeman Art Library; Corbis: 65 © Viviane Moos, 148 © Cooper Andrew; 80 © Dave Coverly/Creators Syndicate; 115 © Getty Images/Hulton Archive; 78 Courtesy of Iarnród Éireann; 10, 109, 111 © Imagefile Ireland; The Kobal Collection: 83 © Renaissance Films/BBC/Curzon Films, 87 © Sam Goldwyn/Renaissance Films/BBC/Coote, Clive; 104 © 20th Century Fox/Morton, Merrick; 50 © James P. Blair/National Geographic Image Collection; 74 Courtesy of Nissan Ireland; 29 © *The Press Democrat*/Annie Wells; 54, 58 © Rex Features; 66 © *San Francisco Chronicle*/Deanne Fitzmaurice; 71 © 2006 Viacom International Inc. All Rights Reserved. Created by Stephen Hillenburg; 144 *Point Blanc* by Anthony Horowitz, published by Walker Books Ltd.

Introduction

This book is a practical guide to the Junior Certificate Higher Level English exam. The chapters follow the sequence of the questions on Paper 1 and Paper 2.

Each chapter includes an outline of the topic, several examples of Junior Certificate questions, guidelines for writing your own answers and model answers.

This exam requires students to focus on the nature of the question and to stick closely to the tasks they are given. Many questions demand that you read a text and respond to comprehension style questions. For this reason, the basic skill is the same whether you are doing the Reading question in Paper 1 or the Unseen Poetry in Paper 2. In each case it is vital to make a point relevant to the question, support it with appropriate detail, a quotation or reference, and explain or develop your idea.

Paper 2 examines drama, poetry and fiction where you must be able to write well about stories and poems you have learned in class. This book will give you useful advice about how to revise these well, in order to write well about them in the exam.

Remember the English exam tests good writing, and good writing is all about paying attention to language. The Lithuanian poet Tomas Venclova says 'Above all, though it's difficult, love language.' We need language to help us make sense of our world and our language is always growing and changing. There are indeed difficulties for you to overcome as you struggle to express yourself, but the effort to improve your grasp of language will yield rich rewards. One reward is success in your exam and this book will help you to achieve the best grade you can in Junior Certificate English.

Section 1 Reading

The first section on Junior Certificate English Paper 1 is the section entitled Reading. As the name suggests this question will test your ability to use the skills of reading, understanding and writing. The passage is usually non-fiction and the topic being discussed will set the tone of the paper in general. For this reason, you should always approach the Reading question first. There may be certain ideas or feelings discussed in the article which will provide a title for the Personal Writing question later on. Obviously the composition titles will make more sense to you once you have read and answered the questions on the passage.

It is recommended that you spend thirty minutes on the Reading question. Read with a coloured pen and highlight key words or phrases as you read. Then read the questions carefully once again marking the key words in each question.

When you have read the question it is vital to think carefully about exactly what you are being asked. Sometimes a key word, or indeed a whole phrase, will alert you to the place in the passage where your answer will be drawn from.

The essential elements of a good comprehension answer are: to focus sharply on the question, to quote in support of your answer and to explain in your own words. A good rule is that three relevant points well supported by examples from the passage and clearly explained is sufficient for high marks.

You should always pay attention to the amount of marks being awarded for each part of the Reading question. It is important to divide your time on the basis of the marks available for each answer. Usually four questions will be asked and all four parts are awarded equal marks.

There are 40 marks for the Reading question. Do not spend more time than this on the Reading question otherwise you will run out of time later on in the paper.

What follows is a series of Reading questions and one question from a previous Junior Certificate exam paper. You should attempt as many of these as possible in order to practise for your exam. To help you I have given model answers to the first sample question and to the Junior Certificate exam question.

A   Read the article 'Darling, Don't Do That' by Tim Dowling and answer the four questions which follow it.

Darling, Don't Do That

Tim Dowling

By normal decent standards, young children are hideously disgusting. It takes discipline to suppress the feelings of revulsion that their personal habits provoke.

As a parent, you must learn that no matter what state your children are in, you still have to pick them up, kiss them and hold their grubby little hands. You must love them unconditionally, even when they're sick on you. Even when they give you lice.

On the whole, children under the age of six prefer to be sticky. They just don't feel right leaving the house without an all over coating of yoghurt, juice, jam, chocolate or another substance.

You can tell that little children enjoy being filthy by the fuss they kick up whenever you try to make them clean. Nothing fills them with horror like the sight of a soapy J-Cloth.

And why shouldn't they enjoy messiness? They live in a world where walking around with a lollipop in your hair doesn't necessarily put you at a social disadvantage. Other children never seem to mind that their companions are so grubby.

The awful thing is that their filthiness rubs off on you – literally. My own standards of what constitutes a clean shirt have dropped alarmingly. Being flecked with someone else's breakfast is now my normal state. I no longer shudder when my boys wipe their bogies on my jumper. I consider it progress that they're wiping their noses at all.

Of course, the real no-go area is

the place they call their own – the back seat of the car. This raisin-studded, rubbish-strewn hellhole is generally not worth cleaning. The seat belts are stiff with grime, the seats are damp and the door wells are tightly packed with half-eaten apples, old sweets and crisp dust.

Perhaps the most irritating thing about children is that they combine their love of filth with an irrational squeamishness.

'I can't eat this chicken,' one of mine will say. 'It's touching spinach.' Yet I have seen this same son eat cat food!

Likewise my three-year-old will not allow anyone to handle his precious bedside collection of old bananas. Even rearranging them slightly brings howls of disapproval. I tend to look on the bright side, and hope that this daintiness will one day develop into a sense of personal hygiene. In the meantime, I'm not holding my breath. Neither am I holding my nose.

Questions
1 How does Dowling prove that children enjoy being dirty?
2 Describe the tone of this piece.
3 Comment on the author's use of imagery and colloquial language.
4 How does the use of humour add to this article?

SAMPLE ANSWERS

Answer 1

Dowling gives several examples of children who seem not to mind being dirty. He tells us how his own children often have a 'coating of yoghurt, juice, jam' or 'chocolate'. This is evidence of a fondness for being 'sticky' rather than being clean.

Dowling's children do not object to this stickiness in themselves or others but they do hate being cleaned. According to the writer nothing can fill 'them with horror like the sight of a soapy J-Cloth'. When he tries to wash them the 'fuss they kick up' shows how they would prefer to remain dirty.

On the other hand they don't seem to object to the condition of the back car seat they frequent. This place is a 'rubbish-strewn hellhole'. Dowling leaves us in no doubt that a great deal of discarded dirt litters their back seat.

All of Dowling's evidence is drawn from experiences with his own children. He assumes that since his children are 'hideous' then all other children are the same.

Answer 2

The passage begins with a tone of revulsion. Dowling says young children are 'hideously disgusting'. The article is full of revolting images, for example 'the seat belts are stiff with grime'. This man seems to be shocked that children can be filthy in so many ways.

Later on, he expresses his acceptance of the fact that his children are dirty and that this affects his own hygiene. When he says that being 'flecked with someone else's breakfast is now my normal state', we sense that Dowling is resigned to his fate as the contaminated Dad of such mucky children. He has come to terms with the fact that his 'boys wipe their bogies' on his jumper. His outrage and horror has been replaced with humorous submission and he cheerfully admits that he now considers it 'progress that they're wiping their noses at all'. We begin to wonder if he was ever truly upset.

Ultimately there is a tone of pride and even affection for his children. The writer still believes that he must love his children 'unconditionally.' Even though he lists their foul behaviour he admits that he still picks them up, kisses them and holds their 'grubby' little hands.

Answer 3

The images in the article appeal to our senses. Dowling gives us several hideous pictures to consider; my favourite is of his children wiping their 'bogies' on his jumper. He uses three adjectives to describe the back seat of the car as a 'raisin-studded, rubbish-strewn hellhole'. The visual effect is clear and disgusting.

There are also many images appealing to our sense of touch. When he says you must love your kids 'even when they give you lice' my scalp begins to itch immediately. Another feeling is the sensation evoked by 'half-eaten apples, old sweets and crisp dust' in the door well of the car. This image manages to conjure up both the touch of these discarded foods and the awful mixture of smells I associate with them.

He uses colloquial language because he is, after all, describing children. Instead of mucus they wipe 'bogies', their dirty hands are 'grubby' and the car seat is a 'no-go area'. More formal vocabulary would be unsuitable and far less funny!

Answer 4

The writer includes several examples of humour in this article. He seems to be making a serious point about how important it is to always love your children until he says even 'when they're sick on you' and 'give you lice'. These comical examples change the mood instantly.

Most of the comedy arises from the way he describes the behaviour of the children.

One example is of 'how walking around with a lollipop in your hair' doesn't bother other children. The idea of children behaving like this is humorous to me. It's also funny when he tells us about the child who refused to eat a healthy meal of chicken because it was touching spinach, but bizarrely the same child had been known to eat cat food.

Without the humour this article would be a fairly routine complaint about the hygiene of modern children. The fact that Dowling makes light of his family's behaviour and is even willing to ridicule his own appearance helps us to see that the consequences are not really serious. The idea of children being filled with horror at 'the sight of a soapy J-Cloth' is amusing and enjoyable.

B   Read carefully the following passage from 'A Swim for the Soul' by Róisín Ingle in *The Irish Times* and answer the questions which follow.

A Swim for the Soul
Róisín Ingle

If Brian hadn't come back from Bombay for Peter and Aoife's wedding I would never have known what it was like to swim with a dolphin. Brian, known variously as Yoga Boy or Siddhartha to his friends, is the kind of brother who comes rushing over to your apartment and says: 'Oh my god, man, guess what, there is a dolphin swimming in the exact place on the west coast where you nearly drowned. We are totally going to swim with that dolphin. Biba says it has healing powers, man. It's meant to be. We have got to check it out.'

For reasons entirely to do with Brian's arrival in the Western world, my resistance was already low and I knew that trying to change his mind on this one would be pointless. The same week he had more or less frog-marched me to the East Wall Community Centre where I was introduced to his newly invented form of yoga. I'll be the first to admit those three days of Soma yoga were an edifying experience, both for body and mind, but after a few too many Downward Dogs (don't ask) this yoga novice felt dog rough. And I just didn't have the energy to argue.

So I meekly accepted the fact that on the first Sunday in October, we were going to be driven by another yoga teacher, Biba, to Fanore in County Clare, where Dusty the dolphin has been delighting observers since she legged it here from her previous hang-out at Doolin.

'That Fungi in Dingle is a bit of a tart,' said Brian, who overnight had metamorphosed from a yoga teaching osteopath into an expert on the personalities of seafaring animals. 'Dusty is the alternative dolphin.'

Apparently that Kerrymaid ad ('a dolphin is a man's best friend, ha, ha, ha, ha') hasn't done poor Fungi's reputation much good. Some non-believers say Fungi probably expects royalty cheques and appearance fees, while newcomer Dusty is like one of the freshly plucked contestants on *Popstars: The Rivals* and hasn't become jaded by all the attention.

The night before the day trip, some family skeletons had been dragged out of the cupboard by Brian and there were lots of tears before bedtime. I had been acting as a sort of mediator during Brian's trip home. We were emotionally hung over as we left Dublin. Dusty named after Dusty Springfield, who had her ashes scattered in the Atlantic, represented the cure.

As Brian had pointed out, I nearly drowned at Fanore in the early 1980s in the days when being bashed about by twenty-foot waves was my idea of fun. I was ten years old and I remember thinking 'This is it, this is the end.' It was dark and we really shouldn't have been swimming at all, Damien and me.

He was a family friend, a father figure really, whom I loved. When I finally reached the shore, I looked back into the sea and he was gone. I hadn't been back since. He was buried in Fanore, just a few minutes away from where Dusty lives now.

We found his grave and I realised for the first time that he was only thirty-four when he drowned. I walked out to the spot where it happened. There is a sign there now: *Bathing is Unsafe in this Area.* Better late than never, I suppose.

We saw the caravan where we waited all night to see if he might come back and make us a cup of tea and laugh so hard his curly black hair would shake. I closed my eyes and imagined him waving from his blue Renault 4. I was so glad I had come.

After that, and a break for what we prayed were dolphin-friendly tuna sandwiches, we were ready to meet Dusty. Brian and Biba wore matching wetsuits. I wore my swimming togs and, inexplicably, a black Prince Naseem T-shirt.

The cove was crowded with boys in canoes and people in boats and children paddling among the rocks. Every few minutes we would hold our breaths as the dolphin flipped out of the water, sometimes far away and sometimes so close you could reach out and touch her.

There was something magical about all these people who had just come to spend time with or to observe such a magnificent wild creature. Even swimming in the Atlantic Ocean, for the first time since the last time, was an incredible experience. I don't know if it was Dusty or the fact that I was returning to a special place I had tried to forget about for too long.

Anyway, as corny as it sounds I felt at peace bobbing around in the seaweed, the sun shining down as Dusty seduced us all. And I thanked her as I got out of the water. For drawing me back there, for reminding me of the good times. Tired, depressed, emotionally hung over? You could do worse than head west for some dolphin-therapy. Like my brother says, it's healing. Man.

Questions
1 What kind of person is Brian Ingle?
2 Do you think Róisín Ingle has a good relationship with her brother? Explain your answer.
3 This is a very dramatic piece of writing. What makes it so dramatic?
4 Would you like to visit Fanore after reading Róisín's article?

C Read the essay *From Bedtime Tales* by Catherine Ann Cullen and answer the questions which follow.

From Bedtime Tales
Catherine Ann Cullen

Morning is wiser than evening, say the Russian fairytales. And rightly so, for how many of our fears are nocturnal – succubi, nightmares, monsters under the bed, vampires – but vanish at first light? Little wonder that our traditional bedtime stories, the fairy tales which give our collective fears shape and form, so often feature beds themselves, and strange bedfellows too.

There's the story of the Frog Prince, where the young princess is understandably loath to take a slimy amphibian under her silken sheets, whatever bargain she might have struck with the creature in broad daylight. Where there's muck there may be brass, but what comes from the river's murky bed is not desirable in the brass one – at least, not until it is transformed into a handsome prince. Princesses are very attached to their fine feather beds, with the sheets turned down so bravely oh.

There's Red Riding Hood, where the wolf hones his cross dressing skills in Granny's nightgown and nightcap, and hops into her bed – all the better to eat a tasty mortal morsel. What big eyes he has, and what a big stomach full of Granny, and what a big stomach-ache when the woodcutter cuts him open and saves the day. The message from such tales seems not to be 'beware of letting undesirables in your bed' but rather that, if they do get in, either they'll turn into princes with a kiss, or they'll be turned on their heels by a woodcutter in shining armour who will happen by just as you scream.

There's the Princess and the Pea, where the possibility of an impostor in the four-poster is so intolerable to the queen that she gives the self-proclaimed princess the ultimate pulse test. Twenty-seven feather mattresses are piled up on one pea, yet the poor princess gets not a wink of sleep all night. She is black and blue with the effort, and next morning the queen is pea-green with envy.

Then there are the Twelve Dancing Princesses, who slip out of the dormitory through a secret trapdoor to dance the night away at an underground party. Bolsters in their beds may give the impression that they are dreaming peacefully, but their worn-out slippers give the lie to their pretence of lying down.

And then there are those who really are asleep, those deep sleepers who wait only to be woken – the Sleeping Beauties and the Snow Whites – lovely and lifeless until they are kissed awake by a prince bending over their glass coffin or their century-old silken bed. Be not afraid, the stories tell us, even of death, for what looks like death is only a long, long sleep.

The strangest of all the 'beds at bedtime' tales is the story of Goldilocks. Perhaps this is the story that bear parents tell to baby bears, because it is Goldilocks the human, and not Daddy or Mammy Bear, who is the monstrous intruder here, breaking furniture, stealing food and terrifying the law-abiding citizens of the wood. It is really not fair at all that she leaps out of the window and gets away scot-free.

My sister and I used to leap from the open bedroom doorway on to our bed to avoid having our ankles grabbed by monsters or intruders. Once on the bed, we had sanctuary from all enemies, as if every wick of the candlewick bedspread was a little nightlight for our protection.

Sometimes there was safety in numbers, especially in large numbers of visiting cousins. Topping and tailing in our house was not confined to fruit, it was what my father called the practice of putting as many children as possible into a bed, by putting heads at each end and pillows, if you were lucky. Your best hope was that your opposite number would be a small child – tall ones meant you got their feet in your mouth and were sure to dream of something unpleasant.

But whether we lay side by side or top to tail, we prayed the same prayer – 'Four corners on my bed, four angels at my head'. And before we closed our eyes, by the light of a nightlight or the crack of light from the door, we identified suspected monsters as a coat draped over a chair or the shadow thrown by a streetlamp.

Then, bolstered by our incantations and our nightlights, we drifted into dreamland. We took comfort in our fine feather beds, courage from the sheets turned down so bravely oh, and consolation from the Russian fairytales, which say that morning is wiser than evening.

Questions

1   Why do you think beds and strange bedfellows feature in so many children's stories?
2   What was bedtime like in Catherine Ann Cullen's childhood home?
3   Based on the passage above what kind of person is Catherine Ann Cullen?
4   Explain the meaning of the Russian proverb 'Morning is wiser than evening' as it applies to this story.

D   Read the article 'What There Is to See at the Zoo' by Marianne Moore and answer the questions which follow.

What There Is to See at the Zoo
Marianne Moore

The peacock spreads his tail, and the nearly circular eyes at regular intervals in the fan are a sight at which to marvel – forming a lacework of white on more delicate white if the peacock is a white one; of indigo, lighter blue, emerald and fawn if the peacock is blue and green.

Look at the tiger. The light and dark of his stripes and the black edge encircling the white patch on his ear help him to look like the jungle with flecks of sun on it. In the way of colour, we rarely see a blacker black than tiger stripes, unless it is the black body down of the blue bird of paradise.

Tiger stripes have a merely comparative symmetry beside the almost exact symmetry of a Grevy's zebra. The small lines on one side of the zebra's face precisely match those on the other side, and the small sock stripes on one front leg are an exact duplicate of those on the other front leg.

Although a young giraffe is also an example of 'marking,' it is even more impressive as a study in harmony and of similarities that are not monotony of sycamore-tree white, beside amber and topaz yellow fading into cream. The giraffe's tongue is violet; his eyes are a glossy cider brown. No wonder Thomas Bewick (pronounced Buick, like the car), whose woodcuts of birds and animals are among the best we have, said, 'If I were a painter, I would go to nature for all my patterns.'

Such colours and contrasts educate the eye and stir the imagination. They also demonstrate something of man's and the animal's power of adaptation to environment, since differing surroundings result in differences of appearance and behaviour.

The giraffe grows to the height of certain trees that it may reach its leafy food. David Fleay, an authority on Australian wildlife, tells us that the lyrebird 'has a very large eye that it may see [grubs] in the dim light of the tree fern gullies in which it lives'. Certain chameleons have an eye that revolves in its socket, as some searchlights turn on a revolving swivel, in order to look forward and back.

The bodies of sea lions, frogs, and eels are streamlined so that they can slip through the water with the least possible effort. Living almost entirely in the water, an alligator is shaped like a boat and propels itself by its tail as if it were feathering a sculling oar.

The elephant has an inconsequential tail, but its long nose, or trunk, has the uses of a hand as well as the power of a battering ram. It can pull down branches for food or push flat the trees that block its progress through the jungle. Helen Fischer, in her photo series 'The Educated Elephants of Thailand', shows how 'up and onto the waiting truck, an elephant manoeuvres a heavy log as easily as we would a piece of kindling'. Then 'after

work, it wades and splashes in a cool stream.'

An elephant can use its trunk to draw up water and shower its back or to hose an intruder. With the finger at the end of its trunk, the elephant can pluck grass that has overgrown a paved walk, leaving a line as even as if sheared by man. It can pick up a coin and reach it up to the rider on its back – its mahout (mahowt, as he is called in India). What prettier sight is there than the parabola described by an elephant's trunk as it spirals a banana into its mouth?

A certain gorilla at the Central Park Zoo in New York sometimes takes a standing leap to her broad trapeze. She sits there, swinging violently for a time, and then suddenly drops without a jar – indeed, descends as lightly as a feather to float to the ground. Walking through the monkey house at the Bronx Zoo, we stop before the cage of an orang-utan as he jumps to his lead-pipe trapeze with half an orange in one hand and a handful of straw in the other. He tucks the wisp of hay under his neck and, lying on his back as contentedly as if at rest in a hammock, sucks at the orange from time to time – an exhibition of equilibrium that is difficult to account for.

The gorilla's master feat – the standing leap to a swing the height of her head – is matched by the pigeon when it flies at full speed, stops short, pauses and without a detour flies back in the direction from which it came. At dusk, four or five impalas will timidly emerge from their shelter, then bound through the air, in a succession of twenty-foot leaps, to the end of their runway. Perhaps Clement Moore had seen or heard of impalas and was thinking of them when, in *A Visit from St Nicholas*, he wrote of Santa Claus' reindeer skimming the housetops.

The swimmer has a valuable lesson in muscular control as he watches a sea lion round the curve of its pool, corkscrewing in a spiral as it changes from the usual position to swim upside down. Hardening-up exercises in military training, with obstacles to surmount and ditches to clear, involve skills neatly mastered by animals. In the wilds, bands of gibbons swing from tree to tree as army trainees swing by ropes or work along the bars of a jungle-gym.

Animals are 'propelled by muscles that move their bones as levers, up and down or from side to side'. The ways in which the movements of their muscles vary provide an ever fascinating sight. The motions of animals are so rapid that we really need the aid of an expert such as James Gray to analyse them for us. In his book *The Motions of Animals*, Mr Gray says that the bear – a browser, not a runner – rests on the entire foot when walking. The horse and the deer – built for speed – rest on tiptoe (the hoof); the hock never touches the ground.

An essential rule of safe living is well illustrated by animals: work when you work, play when you play, and rest when you rest. Watch two young bears wrestling, rolling, pushing and attacking. One tires, climbs to a broad rock and stretches out full length on its paws. The other stands up, strains forward till it can reach with its mouth the ear of the bear on the rock and keeps tugging at the ear as though dragging a hassock forward by the ear. The rester gets up, comes down and once more both are tumbling, capsized and capsizing.

There is nothing more concentrated than the perseverance with which a duck preens its feathers or a cat washes its fur. The duck spreads oil on its feathers with its beak from the small sac above its tail. The feathers then lie smooth and waterproof, reminding us that we too must take time to care for our bodies and equipment. For as much as fifteen minutes at a time, a leopard will, without digressing to another area, wash a small patch of fur that is not sleek enough to satisfy it. It may then leap to its shelf, a board suspended by rods from the ceiling of the cage. Dangling a foreleg and a hind leg on either side of the shelf, its tail hanging motionless, the leopard will close its eyes and rest.

Patience on the part of animals is self-evident. In studying, photographing or rearing young animals, human beings also need patience. We have in Helen Martini a thrilling example of what may be done for young animals by a human being. Mrs Martini has reared two sets of tiger cubs, a lion cub and various other baby animals for the Bronx Zoo.

The zoo shows us that privacy is a fundamental need of all animals. For considerable periods, animals in the zoo will remain out of sight in the quiet of their dens or houses. Glass, recently installed in certain parts of the snake house at the Bronx Zoo, makes it possible to see in from the outside, but not out from the inside.

We are the guests of science when we enter a zoo: and, in accepting privileges, we incur obligations. Animals are masters of earth, air and water, brought from their natural surroundings to benefit us. It is short-sighted as well as ungrateful to frighten them or to feed them if we are told that feeding will harm them. If we stop to think, we will always respect chains, gates, wires or barriers of any kind that are installed to protect the animals and to keep the zoo a museum of living marvels for our pleasure and instruction.

Questions
1   Peacocks, tigers, zebras and giraffes fascinate this writer. Why?
2   Find three examples of the capacity of animals to adapt to their environment.
3   Comment on the language and imagery in this article.
4   Does Moore convince you that zoos are a good idea?

EXAM QUESTION

Read carefully the following passage and then answer the questions that follow.

'Call the usher! The pleasure of movie-going is becoming a pain, thanks to noisy, guzzling, mobile-phone-using talkers, kickers and general pests.' So said Irish Times journalist, Hugh Linehan, in an article in his newspaper. The article appears below in edited form.

Shhhhhhhhh!

Maybe it's because I'm a spoiled snobbish elitist – and that's not something I'm happy about – but I have to confess I'm finding it increasingly painful to go to the movies with the rest of you, the great paying public. It's not because of the cinemas – standards of projection, sound, seating and ventilation have improved out of all recognition over the last ten years – but (and I am sorry to say this) your standards of behaviour seem to be disimproving all the time.

Kickers are a real source of irritation. The kicker problem is exacerbated by the design of modern cinema seats – a kicked seat reverberates right along the row, so that it can be nigh-well impossible to figure out where it's coming from. In the 1970s, they called this Sensurround and people paid to experience it in movies such as *Earthquake* and *Towering Inferno*. Nowadays, you can have your own personal towering inferno as you reach boiling point after two hours of bone-shaking juddering.

Up until recently, the mobile phenomenon seemed to be spinning out of control. Cinemas were buzzing like beehives with the wretched things and some buffoons even had the cheek to strike up conversations on them during the film. There will always be buffoons, but a corner seems to have been turned in recent times. Thankfully, cinemas have now taken to putting reminders on the screen telling people to switch off their phones, and many appear to be doing so. On an electronically related topic, by the way, what sort of benighted fool needs a watch that beeps on the hour, every hour?

I have some sympathy for those who feel nauseated by the smell of warm buttery popcorn which is so much a part of the multiplex experience, but it doesn't bother me that much. If people want to eat wildly overpriced, grease-saturated cardboard, then that's their business. At least popcorn has the virtue of being (almost) silent food – far better than the high-pitched crackle of the jumbo crisp packet or the extended kitchen-sink gurgle of the almost-drained Coke.

To my mind the real problem in cinemas these days is talkers. They're everywhere and they come in a variety of species. One kind can't help giving a blow-by-blow commentary on the movie. They're bad enough, but there is worse. Top of the list come those who just utterly ignore the film in favour of their own chat. Western society has devised countless places where people can communicate with each other, but cafes, restaurants or street corners are just not good enough for these people – apparently not when they can have the added pleasure of spoiling other people's enjoyment.

Then, there are those who think that any break in the dialogue has been inserted by the filmmaker expressly for them to start talking. The minute there is a pause of more than a couple of seconds they launch into conversation. This is not to forget the downright stupid, who spend most of the time asking questions: 'Who's she? What happened there?' By the time they've got an answer they've missed the next plot point, and the whole weary rigmarole starts all over again.

What is the reason for this plague? The general decline in politeness in society may have something to do with it, but it doesn't fully explain the seemingly unstoppable desire to talk when the lights go down. We don't want funereal silence; a good comedy, horror or action movie can be immeasurably improved by the communal experience of seeing it with an audience. People can shriek or laugh to their hearts' content, and there is a real sense of a shared magical experience. After all, we're all together in the cinema … in the dark. And you never know who is sitting next to you!

---

1   Hugh Linehan outlines a number of complaints about cinemagoers' behaviour. List two examples of behaviour he finds particularly irritating.
    Basing your answer on the text, explain why he finds these examples irritating.
    (10)

2   Hugh Linehan describes himself as a 'spoiled, snobbish elitist' in the opening line of the passage. Based on what you have read, would you agree with this description?
    Support your answer with reference to the text.   (15)

3   Basing your answer on the way the passage is written, how serious do you think the writer is in his criticism of the behaviour of cinema audiences?   (15)
    (2004, Paper 1, Section 1, Reading)

SAMPLE ANSWERS
Answer 1
Hugh Linehan is annoyed by the behaviour of people who eat in the cinema. He is distracted by the 'high pitched crackle of the jumbo crisp packet', which prevents him from hearing the film clearly. A similar interruption is caused by Coke drinkers and the 'extended kitchen-sink gurgle of the almost drained' drinks carton. Both types of offender disturb him because the food they consume is noisy, unlike the relatively harmless popcorn eaters who choose 'silent food' instead.

While Linehan rails against the noise caused by eating, he reserves his most bitter venom for a group he labels the 'talkers'. They include people who offer 'a blow-by-blow commentary' on the action of the film threatening to spoil it for other viewers. Worse still are the audience members who carry on a conversation oblivious of the film.

He also finds that a species of viewer will wait for a 'break in the dialogue' to talk. The worst are the 'downright stupid' interrogative talkers who irritate by asking countless questions.

What all these villains have in common is a tendency to create unnecessary noise, which makes it more difficult for a serious viewer to hear what is happening in the film.

Answer 2

I agree that Hugh Linehan comes across in this passage as being a 'spoiled, snobbish elitist'. His argument against a whole range of people is based on the premise that he alone should determine acceptable behaviour for the cinema. He objects to those who kick, use mobile phones, eat or talk as if they were interrupting a private viewing organised solely for his personal pleasure.

When he points out that 'you never know who is sitting next to you' he appears to forget that the cinema is a public performance for which the audience pay a fee. Once I pay to see a movie and comply with the rules of the Cineplex then I am entitled to enjoy the film like all other paying customers.

If Linehan's restrictions were enforced there would be far fewer people in the cinema. 'Buffoons', 'benighted' fools, and the 'downright stupid' currently pose a problem for him and by excluding them he would appear to favour an audience composed entirely of curmudgeonly bores who take films too seriously.

Answer 3

I do not think Hugh Linehan should be taken seriously. He exaggerates a slight problem and suggests that it has reached epidemic proportions and become a 'plague'. One instance of this hyperbole is when he compares the shake caused by a person kicking a row of seats to a simulated earthquake.

The list of complaints is entirely trivial and the level of behaviour does not constitute a serious 'decline in politeness.' If he were genuinely suggesting barring unsociable behaviour in the cinema then I think he would give examples of truly offensive or rude conduct. Eating crisps and talking are minor complaints and most of us put up with them as a matter of course.

I think the writer is merely letting off steam rather than proposing a serious change in cinema admission policy!

Section 2 Personal Writing

The Personal Writing question is the most important question on Paper 1 and carries 70 marks out of the total 180 for the whole paper. You will spend one hour on this question compared to the thirty minutes you will spend on each of the other questions on this paper.

In order to write a good composition you must understand how to construct proper sentences and paragraphs and how to avoid careless spelling mistakes. Once we have covered these elementary language skills we will focus on how to choose what you will write about in your personal writing. The material you write about is the most important factor when it comes to the mark you are awarded in this section. Your content must be interesting, relevant and original. A good plan will help you to give a clear structure to your composition and enable you to develop what you write in a coherent way.

You will be shown a variety of styles of personal writing and finally you will see how a composition is taken from the initial planning through to developing paragraphs and ultimately to the creation of a complete essay.

SENTENCES

Sentences are the building blocks of all writing. When we communicate clearly we are using words correctly to form sentences. Every sentence must have: a subject, a finite verb, and make complete sense. They can be statements, commands or questions. A sentence begins with a capital letter and ends with a full stop, exclamation mark or question mark.

Forms of Sentences

1   **Subject:** The subject is who or what the sentence is about.

2   **Finite verb:** A finite verb is a verb which has a subject.

3   **Complete sense:** A group of words together must make sense in order to function as a sentence.

Rome is the capital city of Italy.

The subject here is 'Rome', the finite verb is the verb to be 'is', and no additional words or phrases are needed for the sentence to make sense. This sentence is a statement and most of your writing is composed of statements.

Is Rome the capital of Italy?

The subject is still 'Rome' and verb is still to be 'Is'. These six words together have a clear meaning. This time the sentence is a question. Always add a question mark to the end of a question, even a rhetorical question.

Fly to Rome immediately!

In this sentence the subject is implied, but the reader understands that a word such as 'you' has been left out to convey a sense of urgency. The verb 'Fly' is in the imperative mood and the four words together form a coherent command.

There are four types of sentence:
1 Simple
2 Double
3 Multiple
4 Complex

1 SIMPLE SENTENCES

Sentences are simple if there is only one finite verb, e.g. 'Today is Saturday.'

2 DOUBLE SENTENCES

A double sentence consists of two simple sentences joined by a conjunction. There must be two finite verbs.

'Put on your coat and leave at once!'

Each of the simple sentences which together form this double sentence is a main clause. This means that the clause makes sense on its own, e.g. 'Leave at once.'

3 MULTIPLE SENTENCES

A multiple sentence will combine several main clauses to produce a long sentence.

'He shot the sheriff, the heroine fainted and the curtain fell.'

Use double and multiple sentences to give variety to your writing style.

4 COMPLEX SENTENCES

A complex sentence is composed of a main clause and one or more subordinate clauses.

'Once you have poured the wine, you may serve the starters.'

The main clause in this sentence is 'You may serve the starters'.

The subordinate clause depends on the main clause for its meaning and here the subordinate clause is 'Once you have poured the wine'.

Conjunctions are the words used to join up or link the main clause and the subordinate clause:

after	how	until
although	since	when
as	so	where
before	though	while
besides	unless	

Everything you write relies on sentences. If your sentences are correctly written then the reader will understand what you have written. While sentences are the basic units of language, paragraphs are about developing those ideas, explaining, illustrating or expanding them at length.

PARAGRAPHS

A paragraph is a group of sentences with a united purpose. All the sentences in a paragraph are linked by a common idea, theme or concept. When you have explored or developed one idea and are ready to move on to the next, you must begin with a new paragraph. This is essential to give your reader a sense of the logical organisation of the essay. Good paragraphing helps the reader to have a clear idea of the shape and purpose of your composition.

When you plan your composition well it helps to give you an image of the overall arrangement of your paragraphs. At the planning stage you should also think about how you will link or connect one paragraph to the next.

The paragraph usually begins with a key sentence from which all the other sentences flow. Key sentences establish an idea and the subsequent sentences in a paragraph develop, expand, explain or illustrate these initial ideas.

Look carefully at the following three paragraphs taken from the travel book *In Patagonia* written by Bruce Chatwin.

> A Boer gave me a lift back south, through Perito Moreno, to Arroyo Feo, where the volcanic badlands began. He was a veterinary surgeon and he didn't think much of the other Boers.
>
> A frill of pleated white cliffs danced round the horizon. The surface of the ground was blotched with scabs of dribbling magenta. I spent the night with a road gang, whose caravans sat inside a ring of yellow bulldozers. The men were eating greasy fritters and asked me to share them. Perón smirked over the company.
>
> Among them was a Scot with ginger hair and the physique of a caber thrower. He peered at me with milky blue eyes, feeling out affinities of race and background with a mixture of curiosity and pain. His name was Robbie Ross.

The first paragraph deals with identifying the motorist who brought Chatwin to a place called Arroyo Feo. It only contains two sentences, the second of which gives more detail about the man, his occupation and his dislike for his countrymen.

Once this writer changes to describing a place he begins a new paragraph. All five sentences in the second paragraph are linked because they give us information about the landscape of Arroyo Feo or tell us about what happened on the night in question.

There is a change to another new paragraph when the writer begins to discuss one unusual character called Robbie Ross. Every time you introduce a change of character, event, time or location you must begin a new paragraph. This is vital in all compositions whether they are short stories, personal recollections or discussions of topics in a factual way.

Descriptive Paragraphs

In the paragraph below the writer Joe O'Connor is describing a disco he used to attend as a teenager.

> It used to be the last song of the night at the Presentation College disco, Glasthule, where I first strutted my funky stuff. 'Prez', as it was known, was a pretty rough joint. They searched you outside for strong drink and offensive weapons and if you didn't have any, they didn't let you in. But 'Stairway to Heaven' reduced even the most hardened knackers, savage boot boys and nefarious ne'er-do-wells to wide-eyed blubbing wrecks. I can still see it now, a great head-banging mass of denim and cheesecloth and existential angst.

The initial sentence identifies the disco and all the other sentences in the paragraph help that sentence by giving more precise detail. If you are writing a composition where you are discussing aspects of your own experience then you should illustrate your points well by giving clear and accurate examples.

Autobiographical Paragraphs

Personal writing implies that the subject matter and style of your writing in this question should be drawn from your own experience and opinions. If you choose to write an autobiographical or memoir style composition then your material should be drawn from your own direct experience. The following paragraph illustrates this point. It is taken from *Pictures in My Head* the memoir of the Irish film star Gabriel Byrne. In this paragraph Gabriel recreates the detail and sensations of his first trip to the cinema in the company of his granny. Notice how well this paragraph illustrates this experience by reference to aspects of colour and movement.

> All around the foyer there were painted photographs of men with black moustaches and women with bright red lipstick like my mother. Then the sentry pulled back the door and we were in darkness with the noise of those strange voices all around us. We edged our way along by a wall like blind people, me holding on to her coat for fear, till suddenly in an explosion of blinding colour, I saw before me the bluest sea I could ever imagine, and on it two huge boats with sails, sailing under a vast blueness of sky. I turned my head in terror into her body, and for an eternity of moments I dared not look again. When I opened my eyes I saw a light beam in the darkness and a voice asked for our tickets, as it came toward us. And with her arm around me, we followed the dancing light as it lit our way along the steps, 'til we found our seats and I sat down overwhelmed by the fear and the mystery and the magic of it all. But as the wonder grew, the terror died. And so I came to know the lovely dark womb of the picture-house for the first time.

This paragraph deals with the topic of the writer's memory of a key moment from his childhood. The whole paragraph is a development of the experience of moving through the foyer and in to the dark interior of the picture house. Byrne captures the excitement through his attention to the details of sensation and emotion. A relatively brief incident is slowed down for the reader and we are treated to a well-illustrated account of what was happening, what he saw, heard and felt. Ultimately the last sentence gives us a curious image, the metaphor of the cinema as a 'womb' suggesting comfort and security, but also hinting that this was where his desire to act was formed and developed.

Narrative Paragraphs

You will need to be very careful about the paragraphs of a short story. The rule is quite simple, change to a new paragraph every time you switch to a new location, time, event, or character. Every new line of dialogue should begin a new paragraph.

The episode below is taken from a short story called 'Snot's Green Sea' by Frances Cotter. Notice that the extract is made up of nine separate paragraphs.

'After the MP3 incident, I was more tuned into Snot. (That's nearly a joke . . . I think . . . tuned in . . . like on a radio . . . except it's an MP3 player.) I was really keen to know what was on the machine.

Once, in the dressing room, I saw his jacket and slipped my hand in his pocket. I felt the cool, rectangular shape and the two thin leads. I rummaged for the switch and was just about to turn it on, when BANG!

I was on the ground. My ear was bursting as if it was filled with hot chilli sauce. For a second I thought the earplug was a booby trap like a 007 device, but then I saw Snot's white knuckles.

'Don't you ever touch my stuff. Do you hear?'

'But Snot, I just wanted to –'

'It's none of your business!'

His face was very near mine.

'Okay Snot, I was just wondering . . . I won't – '

I was on my feet and running.

The short paragraphs are merited here for several reasons. First of all the change to the dressing room requires a new paragraph. Next there is the paragraph where the central character on the ground is recovering from a blow to the head. Each line of dialogue is given a new paragraph to help the reader to follow the story and realise which of the two characters is speaking. The final line is a new paragraph because a new action or event is happening.

Short sentences and paragraphs are appropriate here as the quick pace of the writing enhances the drama of this episode.

If you write a short story then it should include dialogue. Do not include too much dialogue, a good writer will use reported speech sparingly. Choose a key moment in the story to have characters speak aloud to each other. The exchange of spoken words should be important and remember you do not need to have the characters say everything, often we communicate as much by what is left unsaid.

SPELLING

Many students lose marks because of poor spelling. You can improve your overall grade by spending time learning to spell correctly. The following is a list of frequently occurring words which are often misspelt. Learn to spell each word correctly and check the meaning in a dictionary.

absolutely	breathe	disappointing
accept	brilliant	disaster
accidentally	brought	discuss
achieve	business	disease
across	category	doesn't
address	caught	dropped
although	certain	ecstasy
always	character	efficient
anxious	choose	embarrassment
apologise	clothes	emergency
appearance	college	emphasise
argument	coming	enough
around	committed	equipment
arrange	completely	essential
ascend	concentrate	every
association	conscious	exaggerate
awful	courageous	excellent
awkward	criticism	excitement
background	deceive	exhausted
beautiful	decision	experience
because	definitely	extremely
beginning	descend	fascinating
believe	describe	fierce
benefit	desperate	foreign
between	development	friends
bicycle	different	fulfilled
biscuit	disappear	government

grateful	medicine	received
guarantee	medieval	recognise
guard	might	recommend
happened	minutes	reference
happiness	morning	reign
haven't	mysterious	relief
hear	necessary	religion
height	nervous	repetition
heroes	night	responsible
hospital	nothing	restaurant
humour	nuisance	rhyme
hypocrisy	occasion	rhythm
illustrate	occurred	ridiculous
imagination	office	right
immediately	once	schedule
important	only	scene
independent	opinion	science
influence	organise	secretary
intelligence	original	sense
interesting	panicked	separate
irrelevant	parallel	should
knew	parliament	similar
knight	particularly	since
knowledge	permanent	sincerely
laugh	physical	skilful
leave	pleasant	solemn
leisure	please	something
library	poem	sometimes
licence	possession	sound
light	practice	started
literature	prejudice	still
loneliness	present	stopped
lonely	privilege	straight
loose	purpose	strategy
magazine	queue	success
maintenance	read	surprise
making	realise	sympathy
marriage	really	thought
meant	receipt	together

tragedy	using	weird
tragic	usually	which
tranquil	valuable	while
truly	vengeance	whole
unconscious	vicious	whose
unnecessary	view	would
until	village	write

More Spellings

The words given below include homophones; words which sound the same but have different meanings, and other pairs of words often used incorrectly in student writing, e.g. I would *of* should be I would **have**. Learn how to spell them, check the meaning of each word, and write a sentence for each word using it correctly.

allowed	aloud	
bear	bare	
fare	fair	
for	four	
groan	grown	
here	hear	
higher	hire	
hole	whole	
hour	our	
idol	idle	
its	it's	
lone	loan	
of	off	have
one	won	
pain	pane	
past	passed	
piece	peace	
plane	plain	
purpose	propose	
quiet	quite	
sight	site	
steel	steal	
tail	tale	
their	there	they're

thought	taught	
through	threw	
to	two	too
vain	vein	
warn	worn	
waste	waist	
weak	week	
weather	whether	
we're	were	
wear	where	
weight	wait	
whose	who's	
write	right	
your	you're	

CHOOSING YOUR MATERIAL AND PLANNING

The skill of good writing begins with methodical, clear thinking. When you are given a list of composition titles you must select wisely by thinking about which task suits you best.

Write about What You Know

In order to help you select the appropriate composition answer the following three questions on a sheet of paper before you do the exam. Your answers should be precise. In answer to the first question 'Football' is too vague but 'Arsenal's 2006 Champions League Campaign' is much more valuable to you. Answering these questions honestly will help you to identify the topics you should write about in your exam compositions. This helps to remove much of the uncertainty about this question by planning what you aim to write about before you even see the paper.

- Name three things you feel passionately about
- Name the three topics you know best
- What are your three most lucid memories?

The nine areas you have now identified are all topics you know well because you have experience of them. In the case of the things you feel passionately about, they are aspects of your life and experience where you already have formed strong opinions based on what you know and understand. An example of this could be 'Dangerous driving on the roads of Ireland'. Your knowledge of recent accidents or intense emotions related to your own personal memories of dangerous driving have informed your view, so if you write about it you will be drawing on these experiences to explain your position. The secret to good writing is to think properly about the subject matter and to write about what you know.

Brainstorming

One good way to select content for your composition during the exam is to brainstorm. This is to simply jot down all the words that come to mind when you think of a topic. In the title identify all the key words and list the things you associate with that word or phrase.

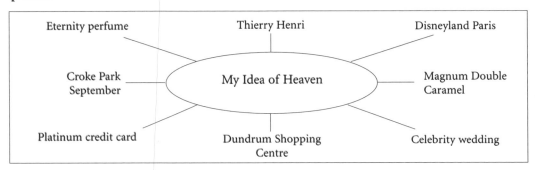

Now look through your ideas and find any possible links. For example, the reference to Thierry Henry and Croke Park are connected and there are two points which appeal to the senses, taste and smell. There are three specific places mentioned, two in Dublin and one in Europe. The last three examples are also linked together evoking ideas of glamour and shopping. Finding associations between ideas helps you to plan where and when to use certain paragraphs. Each new paragraph should be explicitly linked to the preceding one to give a coherent structure to your composition.

Giving Shape to Your Composition

Next you should organise the points in a logical sequence.

1 Introduction: Tell the reader what you aim to do.

2 Body of the composition:
   (a) Heavenly tastes – Magnum Double Caramel
   (b) The scent of paradise – Eternity perfume
   (c) Croke Park in September – Heaven on earth
   (d) An angel come to inspire us – Thierry Henry

(e) Dreamland for children – Disneyland Paris

(f) Consumers on Cloud Nine - Dundrum Shopping Centre

(g) Paying for paradise – A platinum credit card

(h) My celebrity wedding, a heavenly banquet – guest list

3   **Conclusion:** Remind the reader about what you have said.

Each of the items in your list is in fact an example of some aspect of the idea of 'heaven'. The sequence laid out in the plan allows you to develop your composition in a coherent fashion.

The material outlined above represents the body of your composition. This is like the filling in a sandwich. The two slices of bread are your introduction and conclusion. These paragraphs are very important in letting your reader know the approach you have taken in discussing the title.

In the introduction, begin with a strong, confident sentence. It may be a humorous comment, a provocative question or a quotation. Avoid any vague or general banality, make this opening line original and assertive. The next sentence in the introduction will indicate the range or scope of your essay. In this way, you are letting the reader know what to expect in the body of the composition.

The concluding paragraph should draw the points you have made together in a succinct way. The purpose of this final paragraph is to briefly remind the reader about what you have already said.

PLANNING A SHORT STORY

The key to a short story lies in the name. Its shortness obviously refers to the length. In the exam you may write up to four pages of the answer book in the space of the hour available to you. The story is also limited in the sense that you can only really develop one key central character and your plot will build up to a single dramatic moment or climax. There is neither the space nor the time to develop a complex storyline or a wonderfully rich and varied cast of characters.

Setting

Focus initially on creating a convincing picture of a setting, the time and place of your story. Evoke images to help your reader enter the world of your story by appealing to the five senses.

Character

This detailed description of the location should be followed by a development of the main character in the story. First person narratives allow you greater freedom to explore the thoughts and feelings of this person as well as their appearance and behaviour. Once again, pay attention to the specific detail when it comes to building character. Your story will be more convincing if you spend time creating a clear picture of the person at the heart of it.

Conflict

Your central character will encounter a problem and this part of your story is where the main action or conflict occurs. Usually the conflict takes the form of a clash between characters. Here there ought to be a significant piece of dialogue, short but crucial to the climax of the story. The climax is the moment of greatest tension in your short story.

Resolution

From this point on your aim is to bring the story to a clear end by showing some consequence of the climax. Read 'The Ring' by Bryan MacMahon in the Fiction section (p. 131) for a good example of this structure in practice.

USING PICTURES TO BUILD STORIES

The exam question may ask you to tell a story based on a photograph or picture. You are free to use the picture as a launching pad for your short story.

Setting

Think in terms of the information in the picture, about time and place. Pay attention to the details of landscape, weather and buildings. Use the detail to help you in your evocation of the setting of your short story.

Character

If the picture shows a person or group of people then the details of clothing, posture, gestures and expression give you valuable material from which to build interesting characters. Remember in your short story there is one key individual who is at the heart of the narrative. Concentrate on creating a convincing central figure by giving that person a range of private thoughts and feelings. Avoid any tendency to rush into describing a sequence of actions. The plot will be very short and simple as the limits of a short story will not allow you to take on a complex storyline.

Conflict

A picture showing a variety of people immediately suggests the possibility of a conflict between them and this could provide you with the basis of the climax or conflict. You may however choose to invent a separate character outside the frame of the picture who comes into contact with the main character to bring about a conflict. Keep the action simple. Include some dialogue to help create a real sense of drama and contrast.

Resolution

Finally the last part of your short story will show how the conflict unravels. The picture could be seen as the initial moment of the story, the final shot in the narrative, or any key moment in between. A photo is a frozen image of one brief unit of time, the whole story may spring from that scene or lead up to that point. This is where you can be creative and original in your response to the picture.

QUESTION

Write a short story based on what you see in this photograph.

WRITING A SPEECH

One common type of composition is a speech to be delivered on some momentous occasion. The skill here is to write in a style appropriate to your audience and the nature of the occasion. A victory speech delivered by the captain of a county camogie team will differ greatly in tone to a formal debate for or against the motion that *Irish people do not make foreigners feel welcome*. The audience for the second speech are likely to be a more formal gathering and the language and style should reflect this.

Regardless of the purpose of your speech, the techniques of persuasion you will use are the same. Your objective is to express strong personal opinions and arouse intense emotion in your audience. The speech below illustrates this very well. It was delivered by President Bush shortly after the destruction of the Twin Towers in 2001. The speech is analysed for you and various techniques used by President Bush are identified.

Address to the Nation 11 September 2001

'Good evening. Today, our fellow citizens, our way of life, our very freedom came under attack in a series of deliberate and deadly terrorist acts. The victims were in airplanes, or in their offices; secretaries, businessmen and women, military and federal workers; moms and dads, friends and neighbours. Thousands of lives were suddenly ended by evil, despicable acts of terror.

The pictures of aeroplanes flying into buildings, fires burning, huge structures collapsing, have filled us with disbelief, terrible sadness, and a quiet, unyielding anger. These acts of mass murder were intended to frighten our nation into chaos and retreat. But they have failed; our country is strong.

A great people has been moved to defend a great nation. Terrorist attacks can shake the foundations of our biggest buildings, but they cannot touch the foundation of America. These acts shattered steel, but they cannot dent the steel of American resolve.

America was targeted for attack because we're the brightest beacon for freedom and opportunity in the world. And no one will keep that light from shining.

Today, our nation saw evil, the very worst of human nature. And we responded with the best of America – with the daring of our rescue workers, with the caring for strangers and neighbours who came to give blood and help in any way they could.

Immediately following the first attack, I implemented our government's emergency response plans. Our military is powerful, and it's prepared. Our emergency teams are working in New York City and Washington, D.C. to help with local rescue efforts.

Our first priority is to get help to those who have been injured, and to take every precaution to protect our citizens at home and around the world from further attacks.

The functions of our government continue without interruption. Federal agencies in Washington, which had to be evacuated today, are reopening for essential personnel tonight, and will be open for business tomorrow. Our financial institutions remain strong, and the American economy will be open for business, as well.

The search is underway for those who are behind these evil acts. I've directed the full resources of our intelligence and law enforcement communities to find those responsible and to bring them to justice. We will make no distinction between the terrorists who committed these acts and those who harbour them.

I appreciate so very much the members of Congress who have joined me in strongly condemning these attacks. And on behalf of the American people, I thank the many world leaders who have called to offer their condolences and assistance.

America and our friends and allies join with all those who want peace and security in the world, and we stand together to win the war against terrorism. Tonight, I ask for your prayers for all those who grieve, for the children whose worlds have been shattered, for all whose sense of safety and security has been threatened. And I pray they will be comforted by a power greater than any of us, spoken through the ages in Psalm 23: 'Even though I walk through the valley of the shadow of death, I fear no evil, for You are with me.'

This is a day when all Americans from every walk of life unite in our resolve for justice and peace. America has stood down enemies before, and we will do so this time. None of us will ever forget this day. Yet, we go forward to defend freedom and all that is good and just in our world.'

This speech is typical of a style of address given in response to a dramatic moment in the life of a nation. The task of the speech here was to unify the American people in the aftermath of this traumatic event. Repetition is one feature used in a variety of ways. Whole words are repeated; alliterative consonants are another form of repetitive technique, and even the echoing of the name America is effective in reinforcing a clear message. The President seldom uses the first person pronoun 'I' instead he talks of 'we', 'our' and 'us', helping to create a sense of unity between the people and their leader.

Other strategies are employed to generate emotion in his audience. Short emphatic slogans like 'we stand together to win the war against terrorism' express defiance and are used to reassure the people that their country is strong enough to defeat their enemies. Emotive language and buzz words are not used in a logical or analytical way but give vent to intense feelings of outrage or sympathy. An occasion like this is seldom used to reflect in a balanced way, it is more appropriate to appeal to the heart than the head in the immediate wake of a tragedy.

1   **Repetition:** '*our* fellow citizens, *our* way of life, *our* very freedom'. 'America' or 'American' repeated nine times in the course of this speech.
2   **Emotive language:** 'moms and dads', 'evil, despicable acts of terror.'
3   **Slogan:** 'we go forward to defend freedom and all that is good and just in our world'
4   **Parallelism:** 'A great people has been moved to defend a great nation.'
5   **Alliteration:** 'brightest beacon', 'powerful . . . prepared'
6   **Imagery:** 'no one will keep that light from shining'
7   **Superlative adjectives:** 'brightest', 'worst', 'best'
8   **Buzz words:** 'safety', 'security', 'unite', 'resolve', 'justice', 'peace'
9   **Quotation:** 'Even though I walk through the valley of the shadow of death, I fear no evil, for You are with me.'

When writing a speech you should always keep the audience in mind. Address them directly and frequently in the course of the speech. Try to use images to crystallise the feeling of the moment. President Bush used imagery of light to suggest the virtue of the American way of life and to imply the darkness, ignorance and cruelty of their enemies. A good metaphor is very effective in drawing together key ideas and feelings in your speech.

The language register you adopt depends on your audience; a formal gathering requires you to use a suitably serious tone, whereas a speech to family or friends may include colloquial language and a more intimate tone.

Remember speeches aim to persuade the audience by appealing to the emotions. Give concrete examples to illustrate your points and conclude your speech in a confident and assertive way.

Exam question

Write a speech to be delivered to a Third year assembly for **or** against the motion that *Transition year should be made compulsory.* (70)
(2005, Paper 1, Section 2, Personal Writing)

WRITING A PERSONAL DISCURSIVE COMPOSITION

The composition title will sometimes allow you to explore and discuss your personal view of a topic. The earlier exercise above will help you to identify 'what you know' so that you can write well about it.

One other technique is to simply write a list of ten short sentences each beginning with the word 'I'. So a title about hope would mean that you write ten simple sentences each beginning 'I hope'. Try to make the sentences specific. They should include one personal hope, one relating to your family, one focussed on your local area, one hope for the nation of Ireland, one international or global hope. Unpacking and developing these will allow you to gather material for a varied and interesting composition drawing on your individual hopes.

Now arrange these ideas in a plan by finding links between them and imposing a logical sequence or order on your examples. Don't worry if you decide not to use two or three, the remaining points will be enough for a good Junior Certificate composition.

Planning Answers

The composition below by Rebecca Smyth was planned using the strategy of writing ten short sentences each beginning with the words 'I hate'. In selecting her best ideas she decided to focus on four main points and in her essay she elaborates well on these. Notice also the way the initial sentences in her paragraphs establish links between the key examples in the essay. The introduction and conclusion are both short and well focussed on the key idea of the title 'My Pet Hates'.

My Pet Hates
Rebecca Smyth

Pop bands, arachnids, Business Studies, and certain aspects of DIY. 'What do they have in common?' I hear you cry. Well, I'll tell you. I hate every last one of them passionately.

The first one may seem to be a rather sweeping generalisation, so I will clarify that point. I am not a po-faced NME journalist-in-waiting. By no means. I even like the Sugababes! I do, however, really hate the Pussycat Dolls. This group of smirking, scantily–clad, airheads irk me no end. Their music epitomises all that is rubbish in the charts and their attitude is that of all Generation X-Factor. Where once we had Generation X (the lads wore baggy clothes, the girls smelled like teen spirit and their hero was Kurt Cobain), we now have Generation X-Factor (the girls wear barely any clothes, the lads smell like Lynx and their hero is . . . Jodie Marsh!). Although Generation X were hardly the cheeriest of folk, and Cobain wasn't exactly an ideal role model, I sincerely doubt that Jordan is in the running for the *Spokesperson of a Generation Award*. The times are indeed a-changin' when it comes to pop culture.

Far worse than the parasites feeding on the cult of celebrity, are the actual creatures which feed on literal parasites. I mean of course, spiders. They inspire both intense fear and revulsion in me. The worst thing about them is their knack of appearing in the most unexpected of places at the most inconvenient times. The way they move frankly terrifies me. They arch their spindly black legs and delicately crawl along walls ceilings, floors – everywhere. Their habit of bouncing merrily along a silky thread threatening to drop on one's head as they spiral and bumble up and down a web, sends me shrieking across county borders in a bid to escape them. Nature programmes concerning spiders have the same effect on me. The close-ups of their compound eyes, each crackling click of their movements exaggerated, the horrible facts, for example, 'the Goliath bird-eating spider can grow up to the size of a dinner plate', truly disgust me. Don't try to convince me that spiders do a necessary job, or that money spiders are lucky or that small spiders are 'cute'. I've heard it all before and nothing will persuade me that spiders are not super scary, repulsive creatures who would cheerfully eat me alive!

More odious than poisonous tarantulas is the most loathsome of all subjects on the school curriculum, Business Studies! Those two words send a chill of boredom down my spine, tedium so intense that it makes the riff of Coldplay's 'Talk' seem almost electrifying. Not only are final accounts, double-entry bookkeeping and bank statements needlessly complicated, when one of the above doesn't balance, poor put-upon students feel like weeping, tearing their hair out, sending death threats to the author of Business Studies textbooks everywhere or going out to find out what's on the telly. To make matters worse, the course is never-ending and features such treasure troves of information and enjoyment as 'calculating insurance premiums', 'how to form a private limited company' and much more besides! The cherry on the cake is that business is so worthwhile and important – I feel guilty for hating it because it's so necessary to, well, everything. What kind of fine upstanding young lady ready to take her place in the world am I if I don't learn about economic systems? That's right – a happy one!

As you may have guessed, one of the career options I have ruled out is an entrepreneur. Another is anything involving drilling. The incessant whinge of a drill, as it intensifies from low whine to high keen, drives me insane (or up the wall if you'll excuse the building related pun!). The behaviour which drilling entails is also a tad disturbing. Perfectly sane, reasonable, soft-spoken men turn into professionals on spark plugs, plasterboard, faulty elbow joints in piping and other such fascinating 'structural flaws' as soon as they pick up a drill. The journey to Woodie's DIY on a Sunday and the inexplicable desire to buy discount chipboard are other side effects of excessive DIY-ing.

The appeal of 'home improvement' (the euphemism for DIY) is that the drill handler is now alpha-male, taking on all blocked drains, cracked ceilings and suchlike. The flaw in DIY is that the drill bearer is usually a walking liability. Male pride takes over and cries of 'It's supposed to look like that!' abound when one is fool enough to question the large hole in the wall or submersion of the kitchen floor due to a drilled through pipe. The helpful suggestion 'Maybe you should call a builder?' will not be well received. It is taken as a direct challenge to the driller's masculinity. Yes indeed, DIY is truly a mixed blessing.

The only solution to these my pet hates are:

(a) I go to live in a remote, spider free cave, removed from society, devoid of all mechanical drilling devices and copies of *Business Studies for Beginners*.

(b) I get myself deported so that only penguins will have to listen to me complaining.

(c) I take anger management courses. Or perhaps I could express all my feelings in an essay entitled 'My Pet Hates'.

Question

Use the same strategy to plan and write a composition entitled 'Heroes'. To plan it write ten sentences beginning 'I admire'.

QUOTATIONS

Sometimes it helps to begin an essay with a curious, provocative or humorous quotation.

The following is a list of quotations arranged according to themes. Read them and learn any you particularly like. You may find them useful later in composing your introduction to an essay. When choosing a quotation to learn ask yourself whether you have opinions of your own which will help to develop a paragraph beginning with this line.

Over time build up your own store of quotations – a very helpful resource for the English student.

SPORT

'Games are for people who can neither read nor think.' *G.B. Shaw*

'Some people think football is a matter of life and death. I assure them it is much more serious that that!' *Bill Shankly*

'When you win, nothing hurts.' *Joe Namath*

'Swifter, higher, stronger.' *Olympic motto*

'Golf is a day spent in a round of strenuous idleness.' *William Wordsworth*

'Football is all very well as a game for rough girls, but it is hardly suitable for sensitive boys.' *Oscar Wilde*

'He had ice in his veins, warmth in his heart, and timing and balance in his feet.' *Danny Blanchflower of George Best*

'Playing a cheater is a real test of sportsmanship.' *Jack Barnaby*

RELIGION/SCIENCE

'. . . one small step for a man, one giant leap for mankind.' *Neil Armstrong*

'Art and religion are means to similar states of mind.' *Clive Bell*

'Art is meant to disturb, science reassures.' *Georges Braque*

'Science without religion is lame, religion without science is blind.' *Albert Einstein*

'Science is nothing but trained and organised common sense.' *Thomas Henry Huxley*

BOOKS

'A good book has no ending.' *R.D. Cumming*

'Books think for me.' *Charles Lamb*

'If a book is worth reading, it is worth buying.' *John Ruskin*

'Reading is sometimes an ingenious device for avoiding thought.' *Arthur Helps*

'I am a part of all that I have read.' *John Kieran*

'A book is a garden carried in the pocket.' *Chinese proverb*

'The proper study of mankind is books.' *Aldous Huxley*

'A book should teach us to enjoy life, or to endure it.' *Samuel Johnson*

STAGES OF LIFE

'Every man desires to live long; but no man would be old.' *Jonathan Swift*

'Old age is the most unexpected of all things that happen to a man.' *Leon Trotsky*

'The aim of education is the knowledge not of facts but of values.' *William R. Inge*

'Youth would be an ideal state if it came a little later in life.' *H.H. Asquith*

HUMAN QUALITIES

'No one can make you feel inferior without your consent.' *Eleanor Roosevelt*

'He who never hoped can never despair.' *G.B. Shaw*

'Man is the only animal that blushes. Or needs to.' *Mark Twain*

'All sins are attempts to fill voids.' *Simone Weil*

'We are all born mad. Some remain so.' *Samuel Beckett*

'In dreams begin responsibilities.' *W.B. Yeats*

'Human kind cannot bear too much reality.' *T.S. Eliot*

'Love is like the measles; we all have to go through it.' *Jerome K. Jerome*

'We must love one another or die.' *W.H. Auden*

'I have always depended on the kindness of strangers.' *Tennessee Williams*

POLITICAL AFFAIRS

'All human beings are born free and equal in dignity and rights.' *United Nations*

'Money doesn't talk, it swears.' *Bob Dylan*

'Mankind must put an end to war or war will put an end to mankind.' *JFK*

'Injustice anywhere is a threat to justice everywhere.' *Martin Luther King*

'In violence we forget who we are.' *Mary McCarthy*

'When war is declared, truth is the first casualty.' *Arthur Ponsonby*

'There is no such thing as society.' *Margaret Thatcher*

'Politics come from man. Mercy, compassion and justice come from God.' *Terry Waite*

'Knowledge itself is power.' *Frances Bacon*

THE ARTS AND MEDIA

'The secret of art is in life.' *Oscar Wilde*

'If music be the food of love, play on!' *William Shakespeare*

'A great artist can paint a great picture on a small canvas.' *Charles Dudley Warner*

'Where the press is free and every man is able to read, all is safe.' *Thomas Jefferson*

'The medium is the message.' *Marshall McLuhan*

'A good newspaper is a nation talking to itself.' *Arthur Miller*

'You can tell the ideals of a nation by its advertisements.' *Norman Douglas*

'Poetry is a way of taking life by the throat.' *Robert Frost*

'A thing of beauty is a joy forever.' *John Keats*

'A poet is the painter of the soul.' *Isaac D'Israeli*

Proverbs

Proverbs are pithy expressions of traditional wisdom. You can also quote them in your compositions and you may choose to challenge or contradict the opinions they articulate.

> Many hands make light work.
>
> If at first you don't succeed try, try, again.
>
> A watched pot never boils.
>
> Absence makes the heart grow fonder.
>
> Love makes the world go round.
>
> When in Rome do as the Romans do.
>
> A bird in the hand is worth two in the bush.
>
> A friend in need is a friend indeed.
>
> All work and no play make Jack a dull boy.
>
> An apple a day keeps the doctor away.
>
> Never judge a book by its cover.
>
> Half a loaf is better than none.
>
> It's the little things in life that count.
>
> Variety is the spice of life.

FIGURES OF SPEECH

The following terms or figures of speech are used when interpreting or analysing poems, plays or stories. You may not need to use all of these terms, but the list covers a wide range of technical words and offers a short explanation of what each one means.

Allegory: A story or poem with two levels of meaning, one literal level and a second parallel or hidden meaning.

Alliteration: Repetition of consonants, especially at the beginning of words close to each other.

Allusion: A reference in a poem or story to some character or event in another poem or story.

Ambiguity: When a word, phrase or sentence is open to more than one meaning or interpretation.

Anticlimax: When the climax or crisis in a story disappoints or fails to deliver an exciting result.

Assonance: The repetition of identical vowel sounds in words which appear close together in a poem or story.

Ballad: A poem telling a dramatic story in simple language, involving dialogue and action, often with a chorus or refrain usually with a tragic outcome.

Cacophony: Repetition of harsh sounds in a poem or story.

Catastrophe: The death of the hero or heroine in a drama.

Character: A person in a poem, story or drama.

Colloquial: Informal language close to the vocabulary and style of everyday speech.

Comedy: A play or story written to amuse the audience by highlighting the foolishness of people. The ending is usually a happy one.

Conflict: The tension in a situation between characters in a story, poem or drama.

Couplet: A pair of rhyming lines, usually of equal length, in a poem or play.

Crossed rhyme: When a word in the middle of a line of poetry rhymes with a word in the middle of the next line.

Dialogue: Words spoken by characters in a poem, story or drama.

Diction: The choice of words or vocabulary in a story, poem or drama.

Elegy: A poem in which the death of a hero or way of life is described.

Emotive: Language used to arouse intense feeling in the reader or audience.

Enjambment: When the sense of a line in poetry 'runs on' from one line to the next without a pause at the line's end.

Epic: A long narrative tale of adventure usually involving a journey undertaken by a courageous and resourceful hero.

Eponymous: When the name or the hero or heroine is also the title of the story, e.g. *Romeo and Juliet*.

Euphony: The repetition of pleasant or sweet sounds in a poem, story or play.

Fable: A very short story usually involving animal characters whose actions and attitudes resemble human characteristics. They often have a moral lesson for us to learn.

Fiction: Invented or 'made up' stories, poems or plays.

Genre: The type or category a story fits into, e.g. thriller, comedy or horror.

Hero/heroine: The central character in a story, poem or play, usually a noble person who saves the day.

Hyperbole: Exaggeration for the sake of emphasis.

Imagery: The images or mental pictures created by a writer in a poem, story or play.

Interior monologue: When the thoughts of a character in a story, poem or play are written down directly without any break or interruption.

Irony: When there is a contrast between what a character says or does and what is actually the case.

Lament: A sad poem expressing deep regret over the loss or death of a loved one.

Legend: A story passed down from ancient times involving superhuman, heroic deeds and mythical creatures.

Logo: A symbol representing a particular brand or company often used in advertising.

Lyric: A short poem expressing the feelings and thoughts of a single speaker.

Masthead: The top of the front page of a newspaper, including the title, price, date and sometimes a motto.

Metaphor: When one thing is described in terms of another; comparison.

Metre: The pattern of stressed and unstressed syllables in verse.

Monochrome: Black and white photography.

Monologue: A speech by one person only.

Mood: The feeling or state of mind created by a poem or story.

Narrative: A story.

Narrator: The storyteller.

Octave: The first eight lines in an Italian, or Petrarchan style, sonnet.

Onomatopoeia: When the sound of a word echoes its meaning, e.g. fizz, plop, slam.

Paradox: A contradiction in a poem or story.

Parallelism: The repetition of words in a sentence to give balance or symmetry, often used in slogans.

Parody: A mocking imitation of a certain style of poem, story or play.

Pastoral: Poems, stories and plays set in idyllic rural settings often featuring characters from country life, e.g. shepherds.

Pathetic fallacy: When something which is not alive is imagined to have human feelings.

Personification: When an object, animal or idea is described as if it were a person.

Plot: The pattern of events in a story.

Point of view: In cinema, or on TV, a shot taken as if it were being seen through the eyes of a particular character.

Prose: Written language that is not written in the form of verse or poetry.

Quatrain: A group or stanza of four rhymed or unrhymed lines. Shakespearean sonnets have three quatrains and a rhyming couplet.

Register: The style of language suitable in a particular social situation – formal for a formal audience, informal or casual for a more intimate audience.

Rhetorical question: A question which does not require an answer, used for the sake of persuasive effect.

Rhyme: In poetry, when two or more words, usually at the end of the line, have the same or similar sounds.

Rhythm: The pattern of sound in a line of poetry, the 'beat' of the line.

Satire: A style of writing which aims to make a person or group of people appear ridiculous.

Scene: In a play, the subdivision of an act, or all the action which takes place in a particular place at a particular time.

Sestet: The last six lines of a Petrarchan or Italian sonnet.

Setting: The fictional time and place where a story is set.

Simile: A comparison using the words 'like' or 'as'.

Soliloquy: A speech in a drama where the character delivers his/her own thoughts and feelings directly to the audience.

Sonnet: A poem of fourteen lines. Italian or Petrarchan sonnets divide the lines into two groups, the octave and the sestet. The Shakespearean sonnet divides the lines into four quatrains and a rhyming couplet.

Stanza: A separate group of lines in a poem.

Stereotype: An exaggerated or unjustified representation of a group of people, e.g. racial stereotypes are unfair depictions of people of the same nationality.

Subplot: A secondary sequence of events in a story or play, usually involving minor characters.

Symbol: An object in a poem, play or story which stands for something else.

Synonym: A word similar in meaning to another word.

Syntax: The order in which words are arranged in a sentence.

Target audience: The specific group which a media production, e.g. an advertisement, is aimed at. Usually broken down by age, gender and income group.

Theme: A key idea explored in a poem, story or play.

Tone: The reflection of the writer's attitude in a poem, play or story.

Tragedy: A drama dealing with a serious issue, involving a crisis for the hero or heroine and resulting in an unhappy ending, often with the deaths of several characters.

Verse: Poetry or a particular line in a poem.

Villain: The principal evil character in a story.

Section 3 Functional Writing

The Functional Writing section of Paper 1 deals with a wide variety of writing styles. You will be given a choice of at least two different types of writing task. It is vital to practise several different types of functional writing. This unit will give you guidelines on writing:

- Diaries
- Letters
- Reviews
- Reports

Good functional writing begins with a clear understanding of the purpose of your writing. A shopping list is written for the purpose of reminding yourself what you need to buy in the shops. It should include all the items you need to purchase. It should also be brief, a lengthy description of the washing powder is unnecessary! Your list may also follow a logical order, for instance the sequence of aisles in a supermarket. When you are sure you know the purpose of the piece of writing ask yourself who the audience is. The example of the shopping list is only going to be read by the person buying the goods. A letter, however, may be personal, intended for an intimate friend, or formally addressed to a business associate, a customer or client. Letters to the editor of a newspaper are potentially read by thousands of individuals and this will influence the style of language and the content of the letter. The audience will determine the register or style of a piece of functional writing. It is important that if you write a letter telling your granny about your holidays in Tenerife that it should read like you are addressing your granny. The marks you get for functional writing are determined by how well you understand the type of writing you have attempted and how that understanding is reflected in the quality of language and content of your answer. Diaries are the most intimate and personal style of functional writing. This is because the audience is usually the person writing the diary and this gives it a more individual and confidential quality.

DIARY ENTRIES

The key point about all diaries is that the writer is first of all recording his or her thoughts and feelings for their own private pleasure.

This gives the diary a direct, intimate power, as if we are listening to the person's own thoughts. It also means that the writer may not need to elaborate or give great detail because the diary is typically intended to act as a form of shorthand reminder of events as they happen.

Often, however, diarists are conscious that, at a later date, others will read their diary. Famous people will publish their memoirs to give the public an inside view of what the life of a celebrity involves. The diary genre creates a sense of immediacy and can supply a behind-the-scenes glimpse of important moments in the diarist's career.

On the other hand, a fictional diary uses the device of diary entries to give a sense of the passing of time in a character's life. A chronological development of the narrative in the first person means that we have direct access to the character's reaction to key events as they happen. We witness the gradual build up to a climax, or even the shock of an unexpected crisis, through the hero's own personal journal.

Irrespective of the precise nature of a diary it must comply with certain key requirements.

- A diary is written in the first person singular
- A diary deals with specific moments in the writer's life
- Diaries are usually dated and the sequence of entries is chronological

Anyone can keep a diary but sometimes the diary has added interest because the author is well known.

You could be asked to write a diary in the Functional Writing section, the Personal Writing section or even in response to a piece of fiction or drama in Paper 2. When composing a diary entry for a Junior Certificate question you should give some thought to the character of the person and why they are keeping this diary.

- Is it to capture the detail of a key event in that person's life?
- Is the writer an ordinary witness to some momentous occasion?
- Is the character a fictional person telling his or her own version of a short story or narrative?
- Is this imitating a real diary based on recent experiences in your own life?

Once you are clear about the purpose or aim of the diary, then you should write a short plan identifying the number of entries and a coherent sequence of events. The register or tone should be informal and personal. Remember the audience for a diary is always the writer first. It must read like an immediate, private reaction to real events.

Three very different diaries are reproduced below. Each one models a style of diary writing which you will find useful in writing your own diary style answers. Attempt the comprehension questions and then practise writing longer diary answers to the functional writing tasks.

A Below is an extract from the diary of Marcella McGahon, a young mother, writing during the early days of 1941.

Marcella McGahon's Diary

Thursday 2 January 1941
Awfully cold. Spent most of the day in bed with headache.

Friday 3 January
Bombs dropped last night in Dublin. Three people killed yesterday. Scalded my leg.

Saturday 4 January
Leg rather sore, resting it all day.

Thursday 9 January
Knitted gloves for Anita today.

Saturday 18 January
Feeling very much better. Can't walk yet on foot. Snowing all day. Very disappointed with cardigan.

Monday 20 January
Not able to go to mass yesterday, dreadfully cold and snowing all day. Very stormy. Jack Byrne here from Portadown.

Tuesday 21 January
Not quite so bad today. Foot much better. Got tonic for Anita. Letter from Julia. E. McGilligan's baby born.

Wednesday 22 January
Lights off today. Called in to see Mary McGahon, not doing well.

Thursday 23 January
Took children out for walk. Went round to see Mrs Meegan.

Friday 24 January
Poor T.F. died today. RIP. Awful day for us all. Wired Julia. Great crowd down.

Saturday 25 January *Conversion of St Paul*
Terribly lonely. Aunt Mary arrived. People calling all day long.

Sunday 26 January *Third Sunday after Epiphany*
Great funeral. Peter in town. Malachy down. All at 8 mass.

Wednesday 29 January
Had hair cut with Louise. Julia made cake. Mrs Collins up. Went to novena tonight.

Saturday 1 February *Partridge and pheasant shooting ends*
Julia here for dinner. Mrs Collins here for tea. Mrs Fitzpatrick's baby died today.

Questions
1   What do you learn from this diary about life in Ireland in 1941?
2   A diary is a private and intimate document written as a personal record of one individual's thoughts and feelings. Does Marcella's diary match this description? Explain your answer.
3   Comment on the writer's style in these diary entries.

B   The following diary entries are taken from a book called *Out of the Ashes* written by Michael Morpurgo. It is the diary of Becky Morley, a thirteen-year-old girl living on her parent's farm in Devon, England.

Out of the Ashes
Michael Morpurgo

Saturday 24 February 2001
I decided I'd waited long enough for Ruby's foot to heal, and that it was time to try

her out again, gently. I had just about enough time to groom her, saddle her up, go for a short ride and get back before dark. Bobs came along with us and we went down to the river and crossed over. The river was still high after all the rain but we managed. She went like a train up through Mr Bailey's woods and it was all I could do to rein her in at the top. She was puffing and blowing a bit, but I could tell there was nothing wrong with her foot. I was in amongst Mr Bailey's sheep and lambs before I knew it. They panicked and scattered everywhere. I just hoped Mr Bailey hadn't seen us.

By the time I'd got home, rubbed her down and fed her, it was dark. I kicked off my boots and called out that I was back. But no one said anything, and I thought that was strange because I knew they were in – I'd seen them through the window as I came past. When I went into the sitting room Mum and Dad were both sitting there just staring at a blank television screen. Neither of them even turned to look at me. I knew they were upset about something. Then I thought that Mr Bailey must have rung up to complain about me scattering his sheep, that they were furious with me. But they said nothing, just sat there. I asked what the matter was. Dad said it very quietly: 'Foot-and-mouth disease. Some pig farmer up north has got foot-and-mouth on his farm. It was on the news. They've had to kill thousands of pigs.'

Thursday 1 March
Some good news. Some bad news. The good news first. At school today Mrs Merton talked about foot-and-mouth disease. She said what Mum said, that foot-and-mouth isn't likely to find its way down here to us in Devon. Last time there was an outbreak, all the cases were clustered together in Shropshire. I told Dad when I came home, but I don't think he was even listening. And there's other farmers worried like he is. On the school bus, I've seen quite a few farms with disinfected straw mats across their farm gates, and there's more and more 'Keep Out' signs. Everywhere you go now the air stinks of disinfectant. Ruby really hates it. She wrinkles up her nose when ever she smells it.

Now the bad news. I had a bust up with Jay. I was just telling her how worried dad was about the farm, and then she says that farmers are always moaning about something. And for no reason she goes on and on about how I had this and I had that and how I had a horse, and how I was spoilt – in front of everyone. And she's supposed to be my best friend. So I said *she* was spoilt because she's got the latest

Imac computer – she's always showing it off to me when I go over to her place. Then she says if I feel like that she won't ever invite me over again. Well, who cares? God, she can be a right cow sometimes.

Monday 5 March
Up until teatime it was a great day. At school Jay came and made it up. She said she'd been a real cow, and I said I liked cows. So we're best of friends again. Then I was sitting in the kitchen having tea when Mum came in from work. She was white in the face and I soon knew why. They've discovered foot-and-mouth on a farm less then two miles away – on Speke Farm, Terry Bolan's place. She heard it on the radio in the car.

Thursday 8 March
My nightmare began this morning. I went out for a ride, just to give Ruby some exercise. We rode down through the Bluebell Wood to the river. The river bank was high again. Ruby was drinking and I was looking across the river at Mr Bailey's farm. It was deserted, not an animal in sight, just crows cawing over the wood, cackling at me as if they knew something I didn't. Suddenly, I knew what it was. The last time I'd ridden Ruby down to the river was before we knew about the foot-and-mouth. I'd crossed over on to Mr Bailey's farm. I'd galloped up through his wood and out over his sheep field. I'd been in amongst his sheep, sheep that must already have been infected with foot-and-mouth disease. I'd come home again bringing the foot-and-mouth with me on Ruby, on my clothes, in my hair. We'd come back through the river, but river water isn't disinfectant. We'd carried the germs with us back to our farm. And I'd gone out with Dad checking the animals. I touched them. I helped him with the milking that evening. I milked Primrose myself. I fed Little Josh.

This is the worst feeling I've had in all my life. Ever since I first thought of what I might have done I've felt cold all over. I've been sick. All I know is what if it happens now, if we get foot-and-mouth, then it'll be all my fault.

Questions
1   What picture of Becky emerges from reading these four entries?
2   Compare and contrast this diary with the earlier example given above.
3   Imagine you are Becky's friend Jay. Now write two diary entries for Thursday 1 March and Monday 5 March.

C *Paul Durcan's Diary* is the diary of a well-known Irish poet. The diary is broadcast weekly as part of *Today with Pat Kenny* on RTÉ Radio 1.

Paul Durcan's Diary

Ballymahon

Last Friday morning at 10.30 a.m., in pelting rain and storm-force gales, I set off from Ballymahon, Co. Longford to drive back to Ringsend, Dublin. As I rode along the road from Ballymahon to Mullingar, I felt a burst of gratitude for being still alive at all on Planet Earth at the age of fifty-seven and, in particular, for being alive at the wheel of a car driving along the Ballymahon-Mullingar road, the R392, on a wild wet morning in May.

There is no more sympathetic road in Ireland than the R392: the Ballymahon-Mullingar road. It's about twenty miles. Almost all of it is as straight as a die but chopped into steep hills and steep dips. Literally, *up hill and down dale* all the way from Ballymahon to Mullingar.

The sides of the road are lined with thousands upon thousands of souls waving in the wind – the white souls of cow-parsley, four, five, six deep; rows upon rows of cheering cow-parsley jumping up and down in the hedgerows either side of the road. Or Queen Anne's lace, as they call cow-parsley in Meath.

And the white souls also of thousands upon thousands of hawthorn trees in blossom, blossoming baking-powder white over all the meadows and ring forts. Such whiteness in the dark eye of the storm! Only last night, in bed in Ballymahon, I read in a book called *Exchanging Hats* that the poet and painter Elizabeth Bishop considered white to be the colour of 'impassioned reassurance'. How about that, then – 'white is the colour of impassioned reassurance.'

The Ballymahon-Mullingar road! The R392! May the lanes never widen you, never flatten you, never take the kinks out of your hair – your up-hill and down-dale ankle-length hair.

And as I drive along, I drive at not more than 35 m.p.h. – a lesson Christy Moore in his four-wheel drive taught me nine years ago in the vicinity of Yellow Furze, his mother's home place on the Boyne between Navan and Drogheda. There is scarcely another car or lorry on the road and, having to head back to Dublin, I want to savour every half-mile of it. I ride through the villages of Moyvore and Rathconrath. Easy and slow I take the crooked bridge over the Royal Canal. And as I approach the hems of the outskirts of Mullingar, the twin towers of its cathedral kneeling to my left, minding its chapels of mosaics of *St Patrick Lighting the Pascal Fire at Slane* and of *St Anne Presenting the Virgin Mary in the Temple* by the Russian mosaicist Boris Anep, he who made the mosaic floors of the National Gallery in London (who, I wonder, was the avant-garde bishop or parish priest who commissioned these Mullingar mosaics?), the penny drops. I should say: the one euro drops.

How fortunate I am to be driving along the most beautiful road in Ireland while five or ten thousand miles away on a remote Pacific island named Saipan the men of Ireland are dragging down the name of my nation – all that scapegoating, all that thoughtlessness – and India and Pakistan are playing nuclear hooligans. The coin lying at the bottom of my well of well-being is the coin of having slept the previous night for the very first time in my life under the roof of my daughter. Life, birth and death have come full circle. She, who once was a child under my fleeting roof in Cork, last night in Ballymahon gave a roof to her itinerant father. Never have I slept so soundly, sleeping under my daughter's roof.

29 May 2002

Questions
1 What evidence can you find in this diary that the writer is a poet?
2 This diary is also the record of a journey. What elements of travel writing does the entry include?
3 All diaries are written initially for the writer alone. How would you know that this diary is also written to be broadcast on the radio?

Write four entries in the diary of a young fisherman. Your answer should be about 200 words in length.

LETTER WRITING

The style of a letter depends on the audience or person to whom the letter is being sent.

Personal Letters

Personal letters, to close family members, lovers and friends will always be written in a casual and intimate style.

- The language should be informal
- The content will reflect the close nature of the relationship
- Your address should appear in the top right-hand corner of the page followed by the date
- The greeting should be appropriately casual or friendly and is followed by a comma
- Begin the body of the letter on the next line directly beneath this comma
- Each new idea or subject means a new paragraph
- Your closing salutation will be affectionate and casual

D   Read the personal letter below and answer all the questions which follow.

Dundalk,
Friday night

My dearest love,

I have just sent to press that last paper I will edit as a bachelor. That is a solemn thought perhaps, but I don't feel solemn about it.

Four days more sweetheart!

I was over today looking for a suitable scarf, and Betsy made me take a pair of gloves as well. She said I couldn't be married without gloves. I can carry them in my hands like Presbyterian shop boys going to church.

Paddy and Mrs Deery sent me a very nice present today. It is a lovely little writing table. I think it is called a Davenport. If you are very good I'll give you leave to write some letters on it.

Charlie tells me he has written Lizzie Jones in such fashion that she may honour us by turning up after all. On Charlie's account I would be glad if she did. He has a lot to learn yet, and he takes her absence as a disappointment. Not that you or I will care much! But Charlie is a good chap, and I'd like everyone to be happy on this occasion.

I am dead certain we'll forget something. I must write out a list tomorrow and check the things off. Half a dozen times I have thought of 'gold and silver' that I have to give you. I'm almost sure that will be what I'll forget at the last minute. Don't forget to enquire about hotels from Mrs O'Reilly. Frank McPartland has been telling me about a cottage that he and Martha stayed at in Glengarriff. If we're lucky we may light on such a building in Wicklow.

Good night, sweetheart. Four more days will see me the happiest man in Ireland and you I hope the happiest woman.

With love, I am darling your own
Tom
XXX

Questions

1 This letter was found in an antique wooden writing desk. Comment on the significance of this.
2 Tom's letter is personal and intimate. Which details establish the personal nature of the letter? Explain your answer.
3 Write a personal letter home as you approach the end of a three-week long, foreign exchange holiday.

Formal Letters

A formal letter is less intimate than a personal letter. The purpose may be to make a formal request, to complain about a faulty product or service, to apply for a job or position, or to respond to an important event. Your audience is a person or group with whom you have a formal relationship.

- The style should be formal
- The content is a matter of some importance
- Your address and the date appear in the top right-hand corner
- The name and address of the person you are writing to should start on the following line aligned with the left-hand margin
- If you use the person's name in the greeting then the closing salutation should be 'Yours sincerely,' followed by your signature
- When you do not use the person's name the letter concludes 'Yours faithfully,' followed by your signature
- The 'Y' of 'Yours' is always a capital letter and the 's' or 'f' will always be in lower-case letters

E   Read the following letter, taken from *Adrian Mole and the Weapons of Mass Destruction* by Sue Townsend, and answer the questions which follow.

Wisteria Walk,
Ashby de la Zouch,
Leicestershire.
October 6th. 2002

Jordan
C/O Daily Star
Express newspaper Group,
10 Lower Thames Street,
London EC3

Dear Jordan,

I am writing a book about celebrity and how it ruins people's lives. I know what I am talking about. I was a celebrity in the 1990s and had my own show on cable TV called *Offally Good*! Then the fame machine spat me out, as it will spit you out one day.

I would like to arrange an interview on a mutually convenient date. You would have to come here to Leicester because I work full-time. Sunday afternoons are good for me.

By the way, I was talking with my father about your breasts recently. We both agreed that

they are very intimidating. My father said a man could fall into that cleavage and not be found for days.

My friend Parvez described them as being like Weapons of Mass Destruction, and my chiropractor predicted that you would suffer from lower back problems in the future due to the weight you were carrying on your ribcage.

It is rumoured that you are contemplating having even bigger implant inserted. I beg you to reconsider. Please contact me at the above address. I'm afraid I cannot offer a fee or expenses, but you will of course receive a free copy of the book (working title: Celebrity and Madness).

I remain, madam,
Your most humble and obedient servant,
A. Mole

Letter to the Editor of a Newspaper or Magazine

Letter pages afford readers the opportunity to express their opinions on topical news stories or on letters which have previously been published by the newspaper. They are different to personal and formal letters as they are intended for a much larger audience. The style of a letter to the editor will depend on the type of paper or magazine, but for the most part they tend to be quite serious.

If you are asked to write a letter to the editor of a newspaper then the following guidelines apply.

- The letter begins with a simple greeting on the left of the page 'Sir' if the editor is a man, 'Madam' if it is a woman.
- Your own name and address will appear at the end of the closing salutation which is simply 'Yours' etc.

F   Read the letter to the editor of *The Times* and answer the questions which follow.

A letter to the editor of a newspaper may also be a letter of complaint as in the case of the letter below.

—FOREIGN RUFFIANS—

Sir – Rather more than three weeks ago one of my younger sons, about 10 years of age, was passing through London, on his way to school, under the care of an elder brother, a sixth form boy at Harrow. The day was extremely wet, and the little boy was carrying an umbrella to shelter himself from heavy rain which was falling. As he was passing up Regent street, near the Circus, about 2 p.m., he accidentally pushed against, or in some way incommoded with his umbrella, one of the numerous foreigners who swagger about the vicinity, with red caps on their heads and sticks in their hands.

The ruffian immediately turned round and followed the child, and struck him from behind a violent blow on the head with the knot or handle of his stick. His brother who was just in front, turned around on hearing the child cry, and having learnt what had occurred followed the assailant, and, fortunately meeting a policemen, almost immediately, identified the man in charge.

The policeman gave every attention to the complaint, but said that, as on examining the child's head he did not find any blood, he had no authority to take the assailant into custody. As a considerable crowd had collected and the boys were only passing through London, and could not stop without great inconvenience, the elder brother thought it better to let the matter drop there: and I do not know that he could have well done otherwise.

The only remedy for such brutality appears to be publicity in your columns, which may put all who have the charge of children in London on their guard against the violence of these lawless men, for the assailant was walking with a companion of his own class.

The violence of the blow is evinced by the fact that the child is still suffering from it, and the medical man who has been called says that it may be some time before he recovers from it. The cowardly and un-English nature of the act will be best appreciated when it is recollected that the man came upon the child from behind, and struck him, without speaking, upon his head, which was protected only by a light cap, and was covered by the umbrella, so that he could not see the approach of his assailant: and, moreover that the elder brother being just in front, not beside the child, he might suppose that the little boy was altogether unprotected.

A Magistrate for the county of Kent.
5 October 1857

Questions
1   Why did the letter writer send this letter to *The Times*?
2   This letter is also a very dramatic narrative. What makes it so dramatic?
3   Write the report given by the policeman into this case when he returned to his station.

REVIEWS

A review is one person's judgement of the merit of a film, book, play, record or performance. It will usually appear in the pages of a magazine or newspaper and it offers the reader both information and a personal response to the work being discussed.

- A good review will give key facts in the initial paragraphs, in the case of a film review these should include the title of the film, the names of the director and key actors and the genre or category to which the film belongs.
- Your review must also outline briefly the central themes or ideas explored and give some detail of plot or storyline. Obviously you should refrain from mentioning the nature of the film's conclusion.
- Highlights or key scenes may be discussed, especially if they relate to the quality of the actors' performances.
- In the case of a performance, aspects of lighting, sound, costume, special effects, music or editing may also be discussed depending on their relevance to the particular work.
- A good reviewer will clearly express strong personal views on the work being reviewed.

Remember: The reader ultimately needs to know whether you recommend the work or advise against seeing it.

G   Read the following film review from *Uncut* magazine written by Joanna Douglas and answer the questions which follow.

Film Review

Bear Naked
Grizzly Man
Directed by Werner Herzog
Starring Timothy Treadwell, Ami Huguenard, Werner Herzog
Opens February 3, Cert 15, 103 mins.

The latest, exceptional documentary from Werner Herzog focuses on Timothy Treadwell who, in 1990, ventured for the first time into the Alaskan wilderness, intending to live among its grizzly bears. He returned each year thereafter, until, in 2003, he was killed, along with his girlfriend Amie Huguenard, at the claws of one of the very creatures he sought to befriend, protect, and perhaps, on some deep, barely acknowledged level, to become. As a onetime waiter, failed actor and recovering alcoholic, Treadwell had reasons to reinvent himself. Yet his quest seemed oddly reckless, even irresponsible.

Was he really protecting these noble creatures from extinction, as he frequently claimed, or simply a dangerously misguided obsessive?

This documentary, taken largely from Treadwell's own videotapes (he was a tireless self-chronicler, shooting almost 100 hours of footage), doesn't reach a conclusive answer. But it does lend his quest a dignity it might otherwise have lacked.

The first time we see him, emoting desperately to camera, the effect is laughable. Fey, rambling, he seems only tenuously acquainted with reality: 'I am a warrior king out here,' he drawls 'I am gentle . . . like a flower, like a fly on the wall: observing, non-committal, not invasive in any way. But occasionally I am challenged, and in that case the kind of warrior must, must, must become a samurai. Must become so formidable, so fearless of death, so strong . . .' You realise this isn't simply an affinity with nature. This is psychosis.

Later, confronted with a slain baby fox, killed by wolves during the night, he is stunned: 'I don't understand,' he murmurs dully – but how could he? If Treadwell's worldview was simplistic, his vision of nature was positively childlike. And this, Herzog explains, is where the two filmmakers part company: 'Treadwell seemed to ignore the fact that, in nature, there are predators. Whereas I believe that the common denominator of the universe is not harmony, but chaos, hostility and murder.'

For Herzog the appeal of this story is obvious: Treadwell is another in the gallery of outsider-savants, an iconoclast to set beside Kasper Hauser and Dieter Dengler in the filmmaker's gallery of flawed quixotic heroes. The 'kind warrior' couldn't have wished for a more sympathetic champion.

Questions

1   What is 'Grizzly' about?
2   Joanna Douglas awards 'Grizzly four stars out of a possible five'. Why does she like the film?
3   On the basis of this review would you go to see this movie? Explain your answer.

EXAM QUESTION A

Write for your school magazine a review of any one of the following:

*   A film or video you have seen recently
*   A favourite tape or CD
*   A play or show you attended

Give the name of the film, video, tape, CD, play or show that you are reviewing. (30)
(1995, Paper 1, Section 3, Functional Writing)

Book Review

Book reviews are similar in style to film reviews.

H   Read this book review and answer the questions which follow.

At Last, a Rival for J.K. and Harry
Endymion Spring
By Matthew Skelton
Puffin, £12.99

Mary Shine Thompson

Mark the names Endymion Spring and Matthew Skelton. Soon they could be as well known as Harry Potter and J.K. Rowling. Skelton's book may even give Dan Brown's *Da Vinci Code* a run for its money.

Already the publishing industry has worked itself into a paroxysm about this book. No less than five publishers bid for the manuscript, and deals in six figures have been cut. The result is that Matthew Skelton, the stereotypical penniless Oxford student (he completed a doctorate on H.G. Wells), has become Skelton the successful author, with a marketable product.

His book inserts itself into a tradition of children's books emanating from Oxford. It was there that C.S. Lewis conceived Narnia, and from there that Lewis Carroll's Alice (of Wonderland fame) sprung. And Oxford has drawn Phillip Pullman (remember Lyra's Oxford?) to it too.

So how good is *Endymion Spring*? After a rather slow start, the book does live up to the publisher's hype. It is unputdownable. Never again will a library appear to be the fusty, dusty backwater of real life.

A boy called Blake is visiting Oxford with his academic mother and his kid sister called Duck. While their mum immerses herself in olde worlde volumes, Blake feels trapped in the dusty air of the college library. Until one day, Blake is running his finger along the shelf and feels something pierce his finger, drawing blood – like a bite.

The book responsible is a battered old volume, with a strange clasp like a serpent's head – with real fangs. Printed on its front are two words: Endymion Spring. Its dragonskin parchment paper is almost luminous – blank, wordless, but with a texture that seems to shine. The paper quivers, as if it's alive. And as Blake looks, words begin to appear on the page – words no one else can see. The book has been waiting 500 years for the right boy; now it must fulfil its destiny . . .

Interwoven with Blake's story is a story centuries earlier in the 1450s of Endymion Spring, a boy who is an apprentice to the printer Gutenburg and who saves a valuable dragonskin book from the evil Fust (the evil in the story gives it a Faustian overtone). Centuries later, when Blake comes into possession of the book the same dark forces will stop at nothing to get their hands on it.

It comes as no surprise to learn that the film rights for *Endymion Spring* have been sold. The image of the letters of Endymion's book curling up in terror, or the battle with evil conducted on a rooftop among the gargoyles and spires, are gloriously cinematic!

Questions
1 What genre or category of story is *Endymion Spring*? Explain your answer with reference to the text of this book review.
2 According to Mary Shine Thompson, what are the strengths of this book?
3 Write a review (200 words) of your favourite book.

REPORT WRITING

A report is a document which presents facts in a clear and logical manner. The purpose of a report is to offer the reader key information on a topic or subject. Simplicity and clarity are the necessary qualities of a good report. The tone is always detached and the point of view is objective.

1 **Terms of reference:** What is the purpose of the report?
2 **Procedure:** How the information was gathered and analysed.
3 **Findings:** The data or facts presented in the report.
4 **Conclusions:** The logical result arrived at in the course of the report.
5 **Recommendations:** Suggested steps to be taken on the basis of the conclusions.

EXAM QUESTION B

The Transition year class in your school carried out a survey of how the students in Third year spent an average of €10 pocket money per week. Based on the figures supplied below write a report on this for your school magazine. (30)
(2002, Paper 1, Section 3, Functional Writing)

POCKET MONEY SURVEY

	Males	Females
Food/soft drinks	3.90	2.40
Leisure goods and services	2.70	1.90
Clothing	1.00	2.40
Personal goods	1.40	2.30
Transport	1.00	1.00

Sample answer: pocket money survey

1   **Terms of reference**

Transition year students in St Fursey's Secondary School, Killinaskully, were asked by the parents association to conduct a survey of the spending habits of the school's Third year students. The average pocket money was given as €10. The aim of the survey is to determine how pocket money is spent.

2   **Procedure**

We surveyed 100 students asking them to reply to the question: How much of your €10 pocket money do you spend on the following areas?

(a) Food/Soft drinks

(b) Leisure goods and services

(c) Clothing

(d) Personal goods

(e) Transport

3   **Findings**

(a) Food and drinks account for most pocket money; 39 per cent in the case of males and 24 per cent in the case of females.

(b) Leisure is the next priority for males as they spent 27 per cent of their money in this area.

(c) Females spent equal amounts on food and clothing – 24 per cent.

(d) Females spend more of their disposable income on personal goods than males, 23 per cent compared to 14 per cent.

(e) Males spent equal amounts on clothing and transport – 10 per cent of their pocket money on each.

(f) Both males and females spent 10 per cent of their money on transport.

4   **Conclusions**

(a) Transport is not a high priority for the Third year students.

(b) Male students spend more than female students do on food and leisure.

(c) Female students give a higher priority to clothing and personal goods than their male counterparts do.

5   Recommendations
   (a) Students are spending too much money on food and soft drinks. We recommend that the school promote a healthy eating week where students can learn about their dietary needs.
   (b) Too much pocket money is being spent on leisure. We recommend that the school gym be made available free for students at appointed times.
   (c) We advise students to consider walking more in order to save the money they currently spend on transport.
   (d) The money saved should be given to Transition year students whose needs are greater due to their maturity!

In addition to diaries, letters, reviews and reports you could be asked to write a short speech or pep talk to be delivered to a team or group. Speeches are dealt with in the Personal Writing section of this book. A short speech like all other functional writing tasks must be written in thirty minutes which is only half the time available for personal writing. The same principles of planning and composition apply.

Section 4 Media Studies

This chapter will guide you through several aspects of the Media Studies section of your Junior Certificate Paper 1. The media permeate our lives in many ways and you should be prepared to address questions on new or emerging aspects of the industry. It is most likely however that photographs, advertising, newspapers or cartoons will feature in your exam and this section of the book gives you general guidelines for approaching analysis of these different media.

PHOTOGRAPHS

Describing a Picture

A question about describing a picture requires organisation and attention to detail. Begin by saying as much as you can about the background of the picture. A picture can be divided into three areas:

- The top third is called background
- The central third is the middle distance
- The bottom third is the foreground

1   Describe the background and make sure to mention the obvious details, such as whether the picture is taken outside using natural light or indoors using artificial lighting.
2   Another simple fact often overlooked is whether the picture is reproduced in colour or in monochrome (black and white).
3   The background will be either rural, depicting a natural landscape, or urban showing more buildings and organised human activity like industry.
4   If the shot is taken inside a building then the background may feature walls decorated in colours, with windows, paintings and doorways. Give precise details without attempting to analyse or explain the meaning of this location. An objective account should contain factual information rather than subjective speculation.
5   The middle distance of a painting or photograph usually includes someone or something which draws the eye of the viewer. If the focus here is on human activity then you must give the number of people, their gender, approximate ages and how they are dressed.

6   You should also mention the posture adopted by the figures. Are they standing, sitting, kneeling, walking or running? Are they facing the camera? Are the figures in the picture interacting with each other? Are there individuals in the light? Perhaps some action is taking place in the shade. Maybe shadows are cast over part of the photograph. Specific detail is paramount here.

7   Perhaps the picture will include people and animals or a group of animals. If so then you should describe their appearance, the number, their posture and actions. Any picture will contain a great deal of information. We often neglect to mention details we think are trivial or of no consequence. In a question where you are expected to give a detailed description then you must make accurate and precise observations.

8   The foreground of a picture is the part closest to the lens of the camera. Your description should make reference to details to the left, right and in the central part of the foreground. There may be people, animals or objects featured. Size, shape, number and colour are all important factual details.

There could be action happening in the foreground involving contact between people or elements in the picture. It is essential to give a comprehensive account, so make sure not to overlook any section of the picture.

QUESTION
Write an accurate and objective description of what you see in the photograph opposite.

PHOTOGRAPH 1

SAMPLE ANSWER
This photo was taken out of doors in natural light. It is reproduced in full colour. In the background is a dark brown metal girder and beneath it smaller metal bars of a similar colour. It is the undercarriage of a vehicle like a lorry. Behind it, in the distance, I can see green foliage which is blurred or out of focus.

The foreground shows a dusty red surface. There are pebbles and finer particles of sand. It is a dirt track.

In the middle of the photo to the left is a wheel. We can only see half of the wheel in the frame. The metal hub is a light grey blue and there are signs of rust. The tyre is also worn and written on the side of the tyre is the brand name 'Firestone'.

To the right of the tyre sits a child. He is leaning on his left hand and both of his legs are curled up to his right. His feet are bare and caked in mud. He is wearing dark brown trousers and a lighter brown or khaki T-shirt with a clean white collar. On his head partially covering his face is a military style peaked cap. The boy has dark brown skin and black hair.

In front of him in the foreground of the picture are seventeen metal tubes. They are spent bullet cartridges and the boy is arranging them in a row with his free right hand. It looks like they boy is playing a game with the empty shells.

QUESTION

Write a clear and comprehensive account of what you see in the photograph below. Your answer should follow the pattern of the sample answer given for the earlier photograph.

PHOTOGRAPH 2

REPORTS AND CAPTIONS

The second type of question relating to photographs asks you to supply a meaning for the action in a picture by writing a caption or a news report. A caption is a line of text which limits the meaning of a picture usually by identifying the subject or person featured. An example for photograph 1 (p. 65) might read 'Boy soldier plays during ceasefire in Honduras'. The caption must be brief and give the reader all essential information.

The Inverted Pyramid

A news report follows the structure of the inverted pyramid. The most crucial detail must appear in the first two paragraphs. Additional facts are given later in the article and finally extra information is left until the end.

A news report will usually accompany a photograph and if you are asked to write a report your first paragraph must answer the questions 'who?' 'what?' 'where?' and 'when?' A good report will give clear information on the action taking place in the photograph without expressing strong opinions. The crucial detail must be communicated in the initial paragraphs of the report to facilitate later editing of the story should the newspaper need to alter it quickly. Later paragraphs will offer analysis by answering the 'how?' and 'why?' questions, explaining the reasons for an event taking place, and suggesting possible future consequences. A good news reporter will try to keep the report objective by sticking to the facts and not taking sides when telling a story.

NEWSPAPERS

The print media questions in the exam focus on newspaper articles. Most people divide newspapers into 'tabloid' or 'broadsheet'. Although the original meaning of these terms referred to the size or format of paper used in the production of the newspaper, it also has connotations of quality. The broadsheet newspapers are associated with quality reporting. This means that people expect a higher degree of accuracy and a less emotive style of writing in broadsheet newspapers. It does not always follow, however, that a tabloid article will be more sensational or biased than a broadsheet one, but the audience for each type of paper has come to expect a certain style in the treatment of the news. Some critics have suggested that all newspapers are becoming more sensational in their reporting of news stories because of the pressure of increased competition.

1 The first task in analysing a report is to determine the accuracy of the factual content. Does the reporter give the vital information?
2 Secondly is the report fair and balanced, or does it reflect some bias on the writer's part? The reader expects an objective account which gives a comprehensive range of information allowing us to arrive at our own judgement of the events.
3 The third step is to examine the nature of the language used. If the writer uses emotive language then there will be vocabulary which tries to evoke a strong emotional reaction from the audience rather than a cool rational response. We must always be alert to the possibility that the writer is manipulating us by using emotionally biased language.
4 It is always useful to ask who the target audience for a report is. Does it appeal to a general readership? Does it require specialist knowledge, does the jargon used suggest a particular age profile for the intended readers?
5 Be critical. Too often we adopt a very trusting approach to stories which appear in the media. If you read carefully then you become aware of underlying assumptions being made in news reports. A good critical analysis will require you to give a strong independent opinion of the quality of an article.
6 You should always support your response with evidence from the article. The verbal and visual components including headlines and sub-headlines are all useful in this regard. Your answer should attempt to explain or interpret any quotation or reference from the text.

A Read the article opposite from the *Irish Daily Mail* and answer all four questions which follow.

Golden Girl Derval is in a world of her own

BY SHANE MCGRATH

Derval O'Rourke arrived in Moscow as an outsider for a medal but is Ireland's newest sporting hero following a thrilling victory in the final of the 60 metres hurdles.

The World Indoor champion was the picture of joy and happiness, dancing for joy and running a lap of honour after being confirmed a winner.

She had to overcome budgetary restraints and a difficult start to her year's training to record one of the great nights in Irish athletics history in becoming only the third Irish competitor to be honoured in these championships.

Yet she was remarkably composed in the afterglow of her win.

'I believed I had the beating of the girls'

'It was a very special moment and I think it's now only beginning to sink in that I actually won the gold medal,' she reflected yesterday.

'I believed in my ability coming here and I felt I had a great chance of winning. I was convinced I had the beating of all the girls I was up against here.

It's been brilliant to get in touch with my family as none of them were here. I'm looking forward to getting home and

'I believed I had the beating of all the girls'

spending time with them because they've supported me so much over the years.'

Her winning run could scarcely have been bettered, breaking her own Irish record in the semi-final with 7.87 seconds and then coming out to claim the gold in the final with an electrifying 7.84 seconds.

The delay before the final's start didn't ruffle O'Rourke, who picks up €40,000 after her unforgettable night in the Olympiysky Sports Complex.

At the end of the race, there was only two hundredths of a second in it with Glory Alozie of Spain taking the silver in 7.86 and Susanna Kallur of Sweden the bronze in 7.87. After crossing the line, Kallur embraced O'Rourke, convinced of the outcome.

'I felt I'd won,' was O'Rourke's confident assertion. 'I can normally have the right feelings about these things, even when there are only hundredths of a second in it.'

O'Rourke's achievement is even more incredible considering her preparations for Moscow didn't run smoothly when she and her coach, Jim Kilty, began their programme last January.

'We went to Portugal for 14 days and things didn't go very well there. At one stage, I felt we were going nowhere and I ended up in tears.

But Jim insisted I keep my head up and said that it would come right in the end – and it has.

He is unbelievably committed and dedicated and is in the gym every morning at six to work with us. He is not a paid coach and does it voluntarily which is fantastic.

He told me before the final to run my normal race and keep the technique and I would do well. Now I want to target the European championships next summer and my ambition is to get a medal.'

Questions
1   Explain why Derval's victory was so special.
2   How does Shane McGrath's language reflect a bias in his treatment of this story?
3   On the evidence of this story, would you describe the *Irish Daily Mail* as a 'tabloid' or a 'quality' newspaper? Explain.
4   Write a letter to the editor of the *Irish Daily Mail* congratulating Derval O'Rourke.

B Read this newspaper article from the *Irish Independent* and answer all four questions below.

WANT TO BE COOL? TUNE INTO TG4
by Samantha McCaughran

Risqué ads, Spongebob SquarePants and Hector O hEochagain have helped all-Irish language station TG4 win 'cool status and this is good for our native tongue', according to media experts.

Through clever programming and innovative formats, the channel has steadily built up its appeal to the under-15s, while late teens and the twenty plus audience are also tuning into the station. And now Fine Gael is hoping to tap into that new young market with a conference on the Irish language. Today's 'Irish in the 21st Century' conference at Dublin's Alexander Hotel includes both national and international speakers and focuses on the Irish language in our schools and society.

This new focus on Irish tallies with signs that after 10 years on the air, TG4 may be injecting new life into Irish. While the station may not be producing a generation of Gaelgoirs, it is watched by younger views in encouraging numbers.

Last year Irish people spent just over 3% of their viewing time watching TG4, not far behind viewership for BBC2 (3.7%) and ahead of Sky One (2.4%).

Advertising agency Saor Communications says that for the first three weeks of February, 6.8% of all TV hours watched by children between 2pm and 6pm on weekdays were of TG4 programmes.

The station is seen as having a trendy image and its advertising recently saw it receiving a rap on the knuckles – complaints against an ad for 'Paisean Faisean' showing a teacher in a raunchy outfit were upheld by the Advertising Standards Association. But this sort of publicity only makes the station seem more cutting-edge and intriguing to younger viewers.

At a cost of €25m a year to the taxpayer, TG4 has had its fair share of critics, coming under fire for the proportion of English-language programmes it shows, as well as its blockbuster movies.

But Irish Primary Principals Network President Tomas O Slatara said TG4 was providing 'an invaluable service' for young students and was helping to put the fun back into the Irish language.

Brendan MacCraith, communications officer with Foras Na Gaelige, said TG4 helps Irish become a living language with a young audience. 'People aren't watching it just to see something Irish. They're watching something which just happens to be in Irish. That's a major breakthrough,' he said.

Hugely popular international shows such as 'Spongebob SquarePants' and 'Dora the Explorer' are on TG4 with Irish voiceovers.

Hector O hEochagain has been hugely popular with teenagers, while presenters such as Gráinne Seoige, who started in TG4, are role models for those who want to succeed in the media.

And if you have the 'cupla focail', the time to use them is anois. From now until St Patrick's Day, anyone with a few words of Irish is encouraged to put them to use during this year's Seachtain Na Gaeilge.

Hundreds of events have been organised. For information on what's happening in your area, log on to *www.snag.ie*.

Questions

1   What signs are there that TG4 is a successful television channel?
2   Who watches TG4 and why?
3   Is this report balanced in its coverage of TG4? Support your answer with evidence from the report.
4   Suggest an alternative headline and subheadline for this article.

ANALYSING AN ADVERTISEMENT

Pictures, photographs and other graphic elements like logos are often used as visual elements in advertisements. Very many Media Studies questions focus on advertising. It is important to remember that all advertising is a form of persuasion. The techniques used to communicate a commercial message frequently involve the distortion of reality or exaggeration in order to sell the product. There are several tried and tested techniques advertisers employ to get their message across. Some of these methods relate to the use of visual elements in the presentation and other strategies involve tricks with language.

In order to discuss advertising it is useful to consider four aspects of this branch of the media: representation, product or service, audience and techniques of persuasion.

Representation

Every advert offers us a view of the world which is biased in some way. Cosmetic commercials usually show close up photographs of glamorous models in their teens or early twenties whose complexion is improved by tricks like airbrushing. Advertisements for cars often show a motorist driving along an empty stretch of road in a picturesque landscape, hardly ever stuck in a traffic jam in a cloud of exhaust fumes!

You should always pay attention to the way adverts can exaggerate and offer a stereotyped image of certain groups of people. Ask yourself who is being shown or represented in the graphic. Does the picture give a false message about gender, race, age or families? If there is a distortion, then why has the advertiser chosen to exaggerate certain features of this group? In the advertisement for Nissan X-Trail a young couple are featured. The man is shown snowboarding on a mountainside while the woman shops on the high street. Clearly the commercial is inviting us to accept a very extreme view of the differences between young men and young women. The assumption is that all young men choose to recreate by engaging in adventure sports while all women spend their free time buying clothes.

PERFECT FOR WHATEVER SPORT YOU'RE INTO

NISSAN X-TRAIL SX
FROM ONLY €31,225*

Whether your idea of sport is shopping downtown or something a bit more extreme, the Nissan X-Trail SX is the perfect choice to satisfy your spirit of adventure. With 16" alloy wheels, automatic climate control, driver & passenger airbags and ABS + EBD all as standard, the X-Trail SX brings a new spirit of adventure to the heart of the city.

Test drive the amazing Nissan X-Trail SX at your local Nissan dealer today.

AVAILABLE NOW FROM ONLY €31,225* FOR THE 2.0 PETROL AND €36,225* FOR THE 2.2 DIESEL MODEL.

More information about Nissan X-Trail SX on www.nissan.ie

*Prices quoted exclude delivery and related charges. Model show is X-Trail Sport Grade.

SHIFT_expectations

Product or Service

Every piece of advertising attempts to convince us of the benefits of a product or service. Some public service messages present us with useful information or warn us of certain hazards which we should avoid. You probably know the series of television ads which discourage underage drinking, binge drinking and drink driving. Whatever the message, all advertising has an objective which is to change your behaviour in some way.

Analysis of an advertisement must focus on the product or service at the heart of the message.

- Identify the product, it will usually be named several times often with a picture of a typical consumer using it
- Pay attention to the location of the product, most ads will highlight it by placing it in the foreground of the picture
- For certain products the camera angle is important as it will determine how the product is shown in the most flattering way

Look again at the Nissan X-Trail. The angle allows us to view the front and the side of the car simultaneously. The photographer chose a low angle shot to emphasise the size and power of the vehicle. As in many ads the colour of the product is echoed in the background and other details of the advertisement. The logo appears prominently on the front grill and this links with the strategic placing of the logo in the bottom right-hand corner. A further connection is established between the copy or text and the graphic by the number plate which identifies the model 'X-Trail'.

Your analysis may concentrate on how the product is being used or how the service is being presented. Usually the ad will adopt emotive techniques to convince us that our feeling of wellbeing or happiness will be guaranteed if we purchase the item being sold.

Audience

Every advert is aimed at a target audience. This is a group determined by age, gender and disposable income. The advertiser will set out to attract a particular group as these are the potential customers for the company's product. Most ads will give us a visual representation of a typical consumer, but often there will be verbal clues in the copy which will help to identify the audience being addressed. The Nissan ad shows a man in the 20–35 age group, it also shows the arm of a woman of a similar age, the commercial links them as a couple and no children or other family members are shown. Also the copy tells us the prices range from €31,225 to €39,225 which limits the target audience to those who can afford the expense of this vehicle. Finally the copy promises 'a new spirit of adventure in the heart of the city' hinting that the ad is aimed at urban consumers.

Techniques of Persuasion

Advertising agencies are highly skilled in the art of persuasion. There are several tried and tested strategies they employ to lure the consumer into purchasing a product or service. Some of these methods are outlined below.

1 **Emotive language and symbolism:** Words or pictures are used to elicit a powerful feeling in the reader. By appealing to our emotions advertisers hope we will overlook the exaggerated claims they make for their product and by it on impulse. A recent advertisement for Lynx deodorant includes the slogan 'Spray More to Get More!'. The clear implication is that your prospects of romantic success increase as you use this product.

2 **Repetition:** Words or phrases are used repeatedly. This helps to lodge the product securely in the consumers mind, e.g. 'Brennan's, Today's Bread Today!'

3 **Rhyme:** This works like a radio jingle establishing the brand in the consumer's mind, e.g. 'Grace. . . Space. . . Pace.' – Jaguar Cars

4 **Humour:** For example, the series of Carlsberg beer commercials each one incorporating the phrases 'Carlsberg don't do. . .' and 'probably the best' and exploring a comical fantasy world of utopian perfection.

5 **Glamour:** The product is associated with a lifestyle of prestige, success or beauty, e.g. the Nissan drivers snowboard in the Alps and shop in expensive boutiques on Grafton Street!

6 **Superlative adjectives:** Features are described in the superlative to suggest that the product is the ultimate in terms of quality, e.g. 'Simply the Best!' – *RTÉ Guide*.

7 **Imperative verbs:** Verbs are used in the imperative to convey urgency and to create a sense of the necessity of buying the product. The most famous advertising command is Nike's 'Just do it'.

8 **Slogans:** Memorable short phrases often repeated in the course of an advertisement, e.g. 'Pleasure you can't measure' – Mars Delight. 'SHIFT__ expectations' – Nissan.

9 **Logos:** Symbols used to represent the company or organisation. Often they are more effective than language because they can be recognised by all nationalities and they have greater power to evoke emotion from the audience. The most internationally recognisable include MacDonald's yellow M, the Mercedes Benz star and the Nike tick.

10 **Colour:** The colour scheme usually ties in with the product or with prominent colours in the company logo, e.g. the cool blues and silver of the Nissan X-Trail are repeated in the surface of the roadway and the shopping bag and the sky in the Nissan Advert (p. 74).

11 **Buzz words:** 'Perfect', 'amazing', 'satisfy', 'choice', 'only', 'more', 'new', 'adventure' and 'heart' are examples of buzz words which all appear in the short piece of text in the Nissan X-Trail advert shown on p. 74. They are chosen because they create intense feelings in the potential customer, usually positive emotions.

12 **Endorsement:** This is where a celebrity is shown using the product to encourage others to buy it, e.g. Tiger Woods wearing a Nike cap or Jennifer Aniston washing her hair with Plenitude Ultra.

If you are asked to write a critical analysis of an advertisement then you will find some of this terminology useful. The steps outlined below will help to give focus to your analysis.

A   Your analysis should identify the product or service being publicised.

B   Next ask yourself what the advert is promising the consumer. Is the product linked to increased popularity, greater health, a sense of security, a glamorous lifestyle, an exciting social life?

C   Now try to determine how these emotions are being elicited. Which key words or phrases are most effective? Is there a link between the words and the images used? What connections are suggested between the product or service and a pleasant experience for the customer?

D   How does the advertisement exaggerate aspects of the real world? Are there examples of gender or racial stereotyping?

E   Who are the people the advertisement is aimed at? Are they certain types of individuals linked by age, gender or social class? Does the advertisement appeal to different groups at the same time, e.g. young parents, small children, older people, students or couples?

C   Look carefully at the advertisement below for Iarnród Éireann and answer all four
    questions which follow.

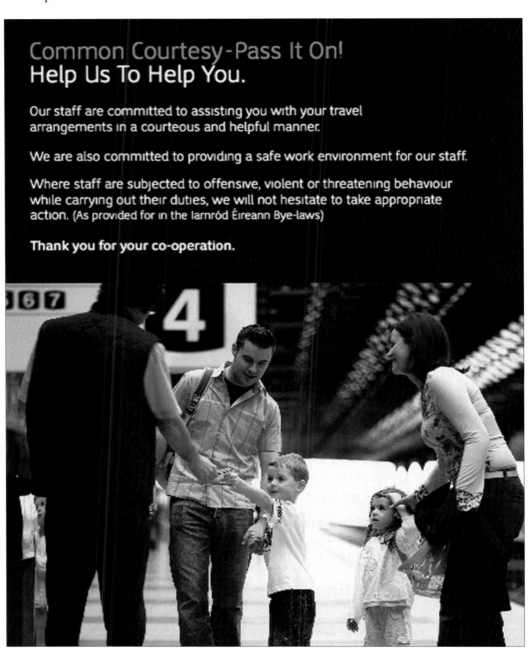

Questions

1 What message does this public service advertisement express?
2 Describe the target audience for this advertisement.
3 What links can be made between the copy or text and the graphic or photograph?
4 Do you think this is a good piece of advertising for Iarnród Éireann? Explain your answer.

CARTOONS

Many newspapers feature cartoons as a regular element of the service they provide. Cartoons are a form of graphic humour and encapsulate a view of news, or some aspect of life, in an extremely efficient way. A cartoon can convey more in one frame, or through several frames in the case of a cartoon strip, than many pages of text or copy. In early 2006 a single frame cartoon appearing in a Danish newspaper gave rise to controversy over its portrayal of the prophet Mohammad. Subsequent demonstrations led to many deaths all over the world. Cartoons are probably the only aspect of the media which is truly international in its appeal and effectiveness, as they are more visual than verbal, and are accessible to many nationalities.

The power of a cartoon to lampoon or satirise its target can also lead to a polarisation of responses from different audiences. Overtly political cartoons have been used to criticise governments and politicians of all persuasions. Less controversial are the cartoons which make fun of common human foolishness. Either way they are an art form which are a popular aspect of the print media and when animated are a very successful element of television programming.

The analysis of a cartoon follows many of the principles of the analysis of advertising. There are usually both visual and verbal elements. The cartoon seeks to exaggerate some comical detail. Sometimes cartoons offer a caricature or stereotype of individuals or groups by taking a perceived trait and highlighting it above other aspects of the subject. Your critical viewing of a cartoon should be alert to this hyperbole or exaggeration.

Secondly, it is worth asking yourself why is this message more powerful as a cartoon rather than as a serious article of a thousand words? Good cartoons appeal to both the head and the heart evoking a powerful range of feelings often arousing several conflicting emotions.

Thirdly, does the cartoon appeal to a particular audience? Like all other aspects of the media there is a deliberate targeting of specific groups and this can be discerned by looking at the style and content of the advert. Many overtly political cartoons are aimed at a more adult audience, while cartoon strips featuring children are sometimes, though not always exclusively, produced with a younger viewer in mind.

D Look at the two cartoons below and answer all three questions which follow.

Cartoon A

Questions

1 What point is being made by each of the cartoons A and B?
2 Which cartoon do you prefer and why?
3 What is unique about cartoons as a form of media?

Cartoon B

Remember: The Media Studies question is the fourth and last question on Paper 1. It carries 40 marks out of 180 for Paper 1 and you should spend thirty minutes on this question.

Section 5 Drama

Junior Certificate English Paper 2 starts with the Drama questions. You must attempt an Unseen Drama question and a question on the drama you studied in class. These two questions carry equal marks.

UNSEEN DRAMA

Shakespearean Drama

LANGUAGE

The unseen drama is divided into two separate questions dealing with Shakespearean drama and non-Shakespearean drama. If you have studied a play by William Shakespeare in class then you may feel confident to answer the Unseen Shakespeare question. Do not be put off by the Elizabethan style of English. Since you have already read and studied a play by Shakespeare you know that it is not essential to understand the precise meaning of every word in order to make sense of a scene. Any obscure or archaic expressions will be explained in a brief glossary.

GENRE

Shakespeare's plays fall into three main categories: tragedies, comedies and historical dramas. Often they explore events of great importance like battles or the death of a king. For this reason the dramatic quality of the story is usually quite clear. There is typically a strong contrast between characters, which makes it easier to discuss the personality and emotions of an individual.

THEME

Shakespeare's themes include the universal ideas of love, revenge, justice, jealousy, rivalry, betrayal, war, marriage and families. All of these themes are reasons to suggest that the unseen Shakespeare play is an option you should seriously consider taking.

CHARACTER

The passage is short and focussed on a key moment from the play. Read the questions carefully and underline or highlight the key words. When you read the passage remember that the paragraph outlining the background to the extract is an information rich passage. It will give you useful clues about the meaning of the scene. You may well quote from this in one or more of your answers. Underline key words in the dialogue as you read. If a question focuses on one particular character then you should pay attention to what he or she says, what others say about them and the actions they perform while on stage. The text in italics is referred to as stage directions and this gives us some idea of when movement or actions should happen. Sometimes the stage directions even reveal how a character is feeling at a particular moment.

Costume, make-up, props

A question about a character may also ask you to make suggestions about how he or she should appear on stage. Look closely at the dialogue for clues about how the character is dressed in order to recommend an appropriate costume. Some characters may require special make-up to exaggerate certain aspects of their physical appearance. If props are mentioned then you should refer to them and how the character carries and uses the props.

Voice, movement, posture

Character is also expressed through voice, so think about the best way to deliver the lines. Tone of voice, volume and pace will be significant elements in the actor's expression of the character's feelings. Posture or stance, gestures and movement are also important in conveying to the audience the meaning of the lines of dialogue. If you mention that an actor should perform a particular gesture then you should support this idea by referring to the relevant lines in the dialogue.

Actors are performing even when they are not speaking, so it is important to think about how the people on the stage are responding to the words and actions of others. The stage directions tell you who is on stage and who enters or leaves during the scene. Always ask yourself who is on stage when a line is spoken and what is that character doing as the words are spoken.

Lighting

When you imagine a scene on stage think about how lights can be used to focus the attention of the audience. Lighting also establishes certain moods or feelings.

Set

The backdrop for the play, furniture, walls or doorways are important in setting the scene. Some unseen questions invite you to make suggestions about how you would use these elements to stage the scene.

It is not always necessary to refer to these aspects of stagecraft, but appropriate, well-supported ideas about how the scene could be played will be well rewarded by your examiner.

A   Read the extract taken from Act I, scene 2 of *King Henry the Fifth* by William Shakespeare. Answer the questions which follow. Guidelines are given to indicate how you should approach answering the questions.

Background to the extract

King Henry has just ascended to the throne of England. During his youth he spent some time in France and enjoyed sport, dancing and going to parties. Now he has inherited the crown he must devote himself to serious issues. His political advisers have told him that he has a justifiable claim to the kingdom of France. In this scene King Henry meets with an ambassador for the Dauphin, the eldest son of the French king and heir to the throne, according to French claims.

King Henry the Fifth
William Shakespeare

KING HENRY:	Call in the messengers sent from the [1]Dauphin. *Exeunt some attendants*
	Now are we well resolv'd; and, by God's help
	And yours, the noble sinews of our power,
	France being ours, we'll bend it to our awe,
	Or break it all to pieces!

Enter ambassadors of France

	Now are we well prepar'd to know the pleasure
	Of our fair cousin Dauphin.
AMBASSADOR:	Your Highness, lately sending into France,
	Did claim some certain dukedoms in the right
	Of your great predecessor, King Edward the Third.
	In answer of which claim, the Prince our master
	Says that you savour too much of your youth,
	And bids you be advis'd there's nought in France
	That can be with a [2]nimble galliard won;
	You cannot [3]revel into dukedoms there.
	He therefore sends you, [4]meeter for your spirit,
	This [5]tun of treasure; and, in lieu of this,
	Desires you let the dukedoms that you claim
	Hear no more of you. This the Dauphin speaks.
KING HENRY:	What treasure, uncle?
EXETER:	Tennis-balls, my liege.
KING HENRY:	We are glad the Dauphin is so pleasant with us;
	His present and your pains we thank you for.
	When we have match'd our rackets to these balls,
	We will in France, by God's grace, play a set
	Shall strike his father's crown into the [6]hazard.
	And we understand him well,
	How he comes o'er us with our wilder days,
	Not measuring what use we made of them.
	But tell the Dauphin I will keep my state,
	Be like a king, and show my sail of greatness,
	When I do rouse me in my throne of France;
	And tell the pleasant Prince this mock of his
	Hath turn'd his balls to gun-stones, and his soul
	Shall stand sore charged for the wasteful vengeance

That shall fly with them; for many a thousand widows
Shall this his mock mock of their dear husbands;
Mock mothers from their sons, mock castles down;
And some are yet ungotten and unborn
That shall have cause to curse the Dauphin's scorn.
So get you hence in peace; and tell the Dauphin
His jest will savour but of shallow wit,
When thousands weep more than did laugh at it.
Convey them with safe conduct. Fare you well.

Exeunt ambassadors

1   Dauphin: French prince
2   nimble galliard: lively dancing
3   revel: party
4   meeter: more suitable
5   tun: cask
6   hazard: danger or part of a tennis court, scores in tennis

Questions

1 King Henry is insulted by the message he receives from the Dauphin. Why is he so upset?

2 If you were directing the actors in this scene what advice would you give to the actor playing King Henry about how to deliver his speeches here?

3 Imagine the scene where the Ambassador returns to France. Write the dialogue between the Ambassador and his master the Dauphin.

HINTS FOR APPROACHING UNSEEN QUESTIONS

1 The first question asks you to identify why the King feels insulted by the Dauphin. The Dauphin has sent both a verbal message through his ambassador and a physical gift.

King Henry is insulted by the words of the Dauphin's, and by the gift of a 'tun' of tennis balls.

In your answer you should pinpoint the precise words which so offended King Henry. Your second paragraph will link these words to the 'gift' of the tennis balls. Look again at the 'Background to the extract' for further clues as to why this present combined with the words of the message would have angered the new king at this time.

Finally, you should give some thought to the fact that the Dauphin is a prince while the man he is communicating with is a king. The difference between their respective ranks is also relevant to this question.

2 Answering the second question requires you to have a good grasp of the character of King Henry. We know from the background information that he is a new ruler whose reputation for the playboy lifestyle of his youth may be a source of embarrassment to him. The introduction also reveals a man under some pressure to claim authority over a 'foreign' land.

His initial lines, directed to his court before the ambassador enters, are full of resolute conviction that either France will come under his control or he will destroy it. Advice to an actor should concentrate on how these lines must be delivered. Aspects of performance include strength, tone, and pace of the speaking voice, posture, facial expression and movement. Ask yourself where the King ought to be as these lines are spoken, how his delivery of the words should reinforce the emotion behind them.

The second speech is much longer and a good answer will focus on how the character and emotion develop as the King becomes more overtly threatening. Is it appropriate for the actor to remain in the same position, or what movements would you recommend? For all directions given to the actor you must explain why these are appropriate and quote from the text of the play the words or lines which support your view.

3 The last question often carries more marks and in recent exams candidates have been asked to write a short piece which continues the story in a different style. Here your ability to comprehend the dramatic situation is being tested along with the skill of writing a short piece of dialogue. If the instructions are open ended then any style of dialogue is acceptable. Do not feel that you are expected to continue the Elizabethan register of Shakespeare. A modern, colloquial conversation between the ambassador and his master would be suitable as long as you capture the difficulty faced by the ambassador. He must bring bad news to the Dauphin and diplomacy would prevent him from telling the full truth. The scene you write will be short as you have very little time, but it could be either serious or comical in tone, and the only real restriction is that it should include at least the characters of the ambassador and the Dauphin and be written in the form of dialogue.

CONFLICT

All drama relies on conflict to generate and sustain the interest of the audience. Unseen passages usually involve conflict like the clash between King Henry and the French ambassador in the extract above.

Sometimes, however, the conflict is not simply between two opposing individuals or groups but within the mind of a single person. The following exam question illustrates this well, as there are a number of ways in which the struggle between opposites is dramatised here.

The following extract (in edited form) is taken from *Much Ado About Nothing* by William Shakespeare. Read the extract carefully and then answer the questions which follow.

Background to the extract

Benedick and Beatrice are discussing Count Claudio and Hero, Claudio's bride to be. Mistakenly, Count Claudio thinks that Hero has been unfaithful to him and cancels their wedding. Beatrice weeps for her cousin Hero who, she strongly believes, has been wronged.

Much Ado About Nothing
William Shakespeare

	Exeunt (all but Benedick and Beatrice)
BENEDICK:	(*With great kindness*) Lady Beatrice, have you wept all this while?
BEATRICE:	Yea, and I will weep a while longer.
BENEDICK:	I will not desire that.
BEATRICE:	You have no reason. I do it freely.

BENEDICK:	Surely I do believe your fair cousin is wronged.
BEATRICE:	Ah, how much might the man deserve of me that would right her!
BENEDICK:	Is there any way to show such friendship?
BEATRICE:	A very even way, but no such friend.
BENEDICK:	May a man do it?
BEATRICE:	It is a man's office, but not yours.
BENEDICK:	I do love nothing in the world so well as you. Is not that strange?
BEATRICE:	As strange as the thing I know not. It were as possible for me to say I loved nothing so well as you. But believe me not; and yet I lie not. I confess nothing, nor I deny nothing. I am sorry for my cousin.
BENEDICK:	By my sword, Beatrice, thou lovest me.
BEATRICE:	Do not swear, and eat it.
BENEDICK:	I will swear by it that you love me, and I will make him eat it that says I love not you.
BEATRICE:	Will you not eat your word?
BENEDICK:	With no sauce that can be devised to it. I protest I love thee.
BEATRICE:	Why then, God forgive me!
BENEDICK:	What offence, sweet Beatrice?
BEATRICE:	You have stayed me in a happy hour. I was about to protest I loved you.
BENEDICK:	And do it with all thy heart.
BEATRICE:	I love you with so much of my heart that none is left to protest.
BENEDICK:	Come, bid me do anything for thee.
BEATRICE:	(*Pause*) . . . Kill Claudio . . .
BENEDICK:	(*Horrified*) Ha! Not for the wide world!
BEATRICE:	(*Angrily*) You kill me to deny it. Farewell.
BENEDICK:	(*Calling out*) Wait, sweet Beatrice. (*Benedick tries to stop her leaving*)
BEATRICE:	I am gone, though I am here. There is no love in you. Nay, I pray you let me go.
BENEDICK:	Beatrice –
BEATRICE:	In faith, I will go.
BENEDICK:	We'll be friends first.
BEATRICE:	You dare easier be friends with me than fight with mine enemy.
BENEDICK:	Is Claudio thine enemy?
BEATRICE:	He is a villain, that hath slandered, scorned, dishonoured my kinswoman? O that I were a man! I would eat his heart in the market place.
BENEDICK:	(*Pleading*) Hear me, Beatrice!

BEATRICE:	Talk with a man out at a window! – a proper saying!
BENEDICK:	Nay but Beatrice –
BEATRICE:	Sweet Hero! She is wrong'd, she is sland'red, she is undone.
BENEDICK:	Listen –
BEATRICE:	Princes and Counts! The goodly Count Claudio indeed! O that I had any friend would be a man for my sake! But manhood is melted into being courteous, giving compliments and having nice speech. There is no honour and truth anymore! I cannot be a man with wishing; therefore I will die a woman with grieving.
BENEDICK:	Wait, good Beatrice. By this hand, I love thee.
BEATRICE:	Use it for my love some other way than swearing by it.
BENEDICK:	Think you in your soul the Count Claudio hath wrong'd Hero?
BEATRICE:	Yea, as sure is I have a thought or a soul.
BENEDICK:	Enough, I am convinced. I will challenge him. I will kiss your hand, and so I leave you. By this hand, Claudio will meet his match. Think of me Beatrice. Go comfort your cousin: And so farewell.

Answer **two** of the following questions. Each question is worth 15 marks.

1 What is your impression of either Benedick or Beatrice from this extract? Support your answer by reference to the text.

2 Based on evidence from this extract do you think Beatrice and Benedick are in love with each other? Support your answer by reference to the text.

3 Imagine this scene is to be staged and you are the director. Outline the directions you would give to either Beatrice or Benedick on how to perform their parts. (2005, Paper 2, Section 1, Drama)

HEROES AND VILLAINS

Shakespeare's reputation for creating memorable heroes or heroines is surpassed only by his fame as a creator of scandalous villains. The unseen Shakespearean drama may include a scene which allows you to explore the heroic or villainous qualities of an individual or a number of characters. Sometimes one person can combine within themselves both the very best and the very worst of humanity.

B The scene below is taken from Act Five of the play *Richard III* by William Shakespeare. Read the extract carefully and answer all three questions which follow.

Background to the extract

Richard Gloucester has risen to the English throne by a combination of skilful political manoeuvring and brutal assassination. In the course of the play he killed many people including his own brothers and nephews. In this scene Richmond and King Richard are preparing to face each other in the final battle. Each man is in his tent at opposite ends of the battlefield of Bosworth on the night before the great confrontation.

Richard III
William Shakespeare

RICHMOND:	Good lords, conduct him to his regiment.
	I'll strive with troubled thoughts to take a nap,
	Lest leaden slumber peise me down to-morrow
	When I should mount with wings of victory.
	Once more, good night, kind lords and gentlemen.
	Exeunt all but Richmond
	O Thou, whose captain I account myself,
	Look on my forces with a gracious eye;
	Put in their hands Thy bruising irons of wrath,
	That they may crush down with a heavy fall
	The ¹usurping helmets of our adversaries!
	Make us Thy ministers of ²chastisement,
	That we may praise Thee in the victory!
	To Thee I do commend my watchful soul
	Ere I let fall the windows of mine eyes.
	Sleeping and waking, O, defend me still! *(Sleeps)*
	Enter the Ghost of young Prince Edward, son to Henry VI
GHOST OF PRINCE EDWARD:	*(To Richard)* Let me sit heavy on thy soul to-morrow!
	Think how thou stabb'dst me in my prime of youth
	At Tewksbury; despair, therefore, and die!
	(To Richmond) Be cheerful, Richmond; for the wronged souls
	Of butcher'd princes fight in thy behalf.
	King Henry's issue, Richmond, comforts thee.

Enter the Ghost of Henry the Sixth

GHOST OF HENRY
THE SIXTH: (*To Richard*) When I was mortal, my anointed body
By thee was punched full of deadly holes.
Think on the Tower and me. Despair, and die.
Harry the Sixth bids thee despair and die.
(*To Richmond*) Virtuous and holy, be thou conqueror!
Harry, that prophesied thou shouldst be King,
Doth comfort thee in thy sleep. Live and flourish!

Enter the Ghost of Clarence

GHOST OF
CLARENCE: (*To Richard*) Let me sit heavy in thy soul
to-morrow! I that was wash'd to death with fulsome wine,
Poor Clarence, by thy guile betray'd to death!
To-morrow in the battle think on me,
And fall thy edgeless sword. Despair and die!
(*To Richmond*) Thou offspring of the house of Lancaster,
The wronged heirs of York do pray for thee.
Good angels guard thy battle! Live and flourish!

Enter the Ghosts of Rivers, Grey, and Vaughan

GHOST OF
RIVERS: (*To Richard*) Let me sit heavy in thy soul to-morrow,
Rivers that died at Pomfret! Despair and die!
GHOST OF GREY: (*To Richard*) Think upon Grey, and let thy soul despair!
GHOST OF
VAUGHAN: (*To Richard*) Think upon Vaughan, and with guilty fear
Let fall thy lance. Despair and die!
ALL: (*To Richmond*) Awake, and think our wrongs in Richard's bosom
Will conquer him. Awake and win the day.

Enter the Ghost of Hastings

GHOST OF
HASTINGS: (*To Richard*) Bloody and guilty, guiltily awake,
And in a bloody battle end thy days!

Think on Lord Hastings. Despair and die.

(To Richmond) Quiet untroubled soul, awake, awake!

Arm, fight, and conquer, for fair England's sake!

Enter the Ghosts of the two young princes

GHOSTS
OF THE TWO
YOUNG PRINCES: *(To Richard)* Dream on thy cousins smothered in the Tower.

Let us be lead within thy bosom, Richard,

And weigh thee down to ruin, shame, and death!

Thy nephews' souls bid thee despair and die.

(To Richmond) Sleep, Richmond, sleep in peace, and wake in joy;

Good angels guard thee from the boar's annoy!

Live, and beget a happy race of kings!

Edward's unhappy sons do bid thee flourish.

Enter the Ghost of Lady Anne, his wife

GHOST OF LADY
ANNE: *(To Richard)* Richard, thy wife, that wretched Anne thy wife

That never slept a quiet hour with thee

Now fills thy sleep with perturbations.

To-morrow in the battle think on me,

And fall thy edgeless sword. Despair and die.

(To Richmond) Thou quiet soul, sleep thou a quiet sleep;

Dream of success and happy victory.

Thy adversary's wife doth pray for thee.

Enter the Ghost of Buckingham

GHOST OF
BUCKINGHAM: *(To Richard)* The first was I that help'd thee to the crown;

The last was I that felt thy tyranny.

O, in the battle think on Buckingham,

And die in terror of thy guiltiness!

Dream on, dream on of bloody deeds and death;

Fainting, despair; despairing, yield thy breath!

(To Richmond) I died for hope ere I could lend thee aid;

But cheer thy heart and be thou not dismay'd:

God and good angels fight on Richmond's side;

And Richard falls in height of all his pride.

The Ghosts vanish. Richard starts out of his dream

KING RICHARD: Give me another horse. Bind up my wounds.
Have mercy, Jesu! Soft! I did but dream.
O coward conscience, how dost thou afflict me!
The lights burn blue. It is now dead midnight.
Cold fearful drops stand on my trembling flesh.
What do I fear? Myself? There's none else by.
Richard loves Richard; that is, I am I.
Is there a murderer here? No-yes, I am.
Then fly. What, from myself? Great reason why –
Lest I revenge. What, myself upon myself!
Alack, I love myself. Wherefore? For any good
That I myself have done unto myself?
O, no! Alas, I rather hate myself
For hateful deeds committed by myself!
I am a villain; yet I lie, I am not.
Fool, of thyself speak well. Fool, do not flatter.
My conscience hath a thousand several tongues,
And every tongue brings in a several tale,
And every tale condemns me for a villain.
Perjury, perjury, in the high'st degree;
Murder, stern murder, in the [3]dir'st degree;
All several sins, all us'd in each degree,
Throng to the bar, crying all 'Guilty! guilty!'
I shall despair. There is no creature loves me;
And if I die no soul will pity me:
And wherefore should they, since that I myself
Find in myself no pity to myself?
Methought the souls of all that I had murder'd
Came to my tent, and every one did threat
To-morrow's vengeance on the head of Richard.

1   usurping: illegally invading
2   chastisement: punishment
3   dir'st: worst

OTHER DRAMA

The second option for you in the Unseen Drama section is called 'Other Drama'. This refers to any form or type of drama other than a play by Shakespeare. In the past there have been plays by a variety of authors of many different nationalities ranging from ancient Greek drama to modern plays set in the present time.

LANGUAGE

As many of the plays in this section are set in contemporary Ireland or elsewhere the language will differ greatly from the style of English used by Shakespeare. Dialogue, if it attempts to be realistic, will imitate the speech of ordinary people. This colloquial style is evident in many modern plays.

GENRE

Language also offers a clue as to the type or style of drama in question. Tragedies will include language which establishes a more serious atmosphere, while the lighter language of comedies suggests a happier outcome to the events explored in the play. Some dramas will include a mixture of the serious and the trivial. This reflects our experience of the real world where funny moments can happen at a time of great trauma or grave consequence.

CHARACTER

Once again, as with the plays of Shakespeare, the language a person uses reveals a great deal about character. Vocabulary and a person's style of speaking help the audience to form a view of the character's own thoughts and feelings.

COSTUME, MAKE-UP, PROPS

You should try to picture a scene as you read it. Imagine the colour and style of people's clothes. Think about the condition of the clothes they wear. Are they worn or brand new, of a poor quality or elegant suggesting great opulence?

Make-up and props help to convey character. The props might also play a significant role in advancing the plot or storyline of the play.

Voice, movement, posture

Colloquial language suggests that the actor will have to adopt a particular accent. We are told that the excerpt below from *Amphibians* takes place in modern day Wexford and the language is colloquial, so performing the play well demands some effort to speak in a special way.

Lighting

The lights help to create a mood or atmosphere for a scene and modern drama is sometimes more demanding in this regard. Think about what is happening on stage and ask yourself what style of lighting would help the audience to relate to what they see happening in front of them.

Set

The backdrop and set limits the world of the story for us. A landscape tells us the play is set in the country, while skyscrapers in the background let us know that the story takes place in a modern city.

Creating tension in the audience

C   The following scene is taken from the play *Amphibians* by the Irish playwright Billy Roche. Read the extract carefully and answer all three questions which follow.

Background to the extract

Amphibians is set in Wexford in the present day. Eagle is taking his son Isaac on a boat trip to Useless Island. He plans to spend the night on the uninhabited island as a way of teaching Isaac about growing up and taking responsibility in the adult world.

Amphibians
Billy Roche

ISAAC:	Look at all the stars Da. Kind of electric stars. Not in the sky Da, in the water. What are they, anyway?

EAGLE:	Phosphorous.
ISAAC:	Phosphorous! I must tell them in school about that on Monday. I bet the teacher don't know about that.
EAGLE:	I'm feckin' sure he don't know about it.
ISAAC:	The size of that big eel boy! That fella'd nearly turn the boat over wouldn't he? Hah? What would ye do if he turned the boat over, Da?
EAGLE:	I don't know.
ISAAC:	Can you swim Da?
EAGLE:	Yeah of course I can swim.
ISAAC:	Can yeh? What's your favourite stroke?
EAGLE:	The Japanese flip-flop. Nothin' moves, only your tonsils.
ISAAC:	Yeah, 'help, help. . .' A full moon hah? Deadly looking ain't it?
EAGLE:	Yeah, yeh'd get up in the middle of the night to look at it sure.
ISAAC:	(*Chuckles*) That's a good one Da. You'd get up in the middle of the night to look at it. You'd hardly see it in the middle of the day would yeh? You should have been a comedian boy!
	(*Pause*)
EAGLE:	There she is Isaac. Useless Island. There seems to be a bit of an auld fog comin' down around her.
ISAAC:	Yeah, its queer spooky looking, ain't it?
EAGLE:	Not at all.
	(*Slight pause*)
ISAAC:	I don't think me Ma is exactly over the moon about all of this Da, is she?
EAGLE:	No, not exactly. Ah she's a bit nervous about it. Yeh see Isaac what she don't understand is that you and me are in our element out here like yeh know. What she don't seem to realise is that this is our what–do-you-call-it . . . What's the word? Domain! But sure I suppose she's listenin' to the rest of them blackguardin' me all the time. I'm not coddin' yeh, for the past twelve months here you'd swear I was committing some sort of crime here just comin' out to work. I mean to say I'm only doin' what I always done. Yeh know? I come out here and I cast me nets and I sit and wait. What's wrong with that? Yeh know? No way am I in the wrong, I don't care what anyone says . . . Yeh know sometimes when I'm out here on me own in the middle of the night I'll stand up and I'll let a bit of an auld shout out of me. (*He shrieks*) I'm not coddin' yeh if anyone was watchin' me they'd have me feckin' certified so they would. But do yeh know why I do that? I do it to let this place know that I'm still here, that

	I'm still around. That's very important yeh know! That way the man learns to respect the place and the place'll respect the man. Me Da taught me that . . . Take a look back at the town.
ISAAC:	Oh yeah . . . All the lights! I wonder where our house is? I think I can see my pigeon loft Da. (*Eagle smiles at him tenderly*)
EAGLE:	As long as you do your best Isaac, that's all that matters yeh know. You must always do your best. And make the most of what yeh got . . . What's that? A seagull flyin' low be Jaysus!
ISAAC:	What do you mean?
EAGLE:	Search me (*He chuckles and sits down again*) (*Pause*)
ISAAC:	Do yeh know somethin' Da, I don't think I ever saw you swimmin' . . . Da?
EAGLE:	What?
ISAAC:	I say I never saw you swimmin'.
EAGLE:	Why should I swim when I've got a boat? (*Pause. Lights down*)

Questions

1 What does the scene reveal about the character of Eagle?
2 The action in this scene takes place in a boat on a river at night-time. If you were the director of this play how would you create this illusion on a stage?
3 'There is gentle humour in this scene but also a feeling of tension.' Discuss this view of the scene.

The next example also employs a very colloquial and Irish way of speaking, but while there is a connecting theme of water and boats the mood is much more intensely sad.

EXAM QUESTION B

The following extract (in edited form) is taken from *Riders to the Sea* by J.M. Synge. Read the extract carefully and then answer the questions which follow it.

Background to the extract

Maurya, the principal character of the play, lives in a cottage on an island off the west coast of Ireland. She has had a long life of extreme hardship. Her husband

and six of her sons, all fishermen, have been drowned at sea. In this scene, she and her daughters, Cathleen and Nora, learn of the drowning of the last of her sons, Michael and Bartley.

Riders to the Sea
J. M. Synge

CATHLEEN:	Michael is after being found in the far north.
MAURYA:	There does be a power of young men floating round in the sea, and what way would they know if it was Michael they had?
CATHLEEN:	It's Michael, God spare him, for they're after sending us a bit of his clothes from the far north.
	(*She reaches out and hands Maurya the clothes that belonged to Michael. Maurya stands up slowly, and takes them into her hands. Nora looks out.*)
NORA:	They're carrying a thing among them and there's water dripping out of it and leaving a track by the big stones.
CATHLEEN:	(*In a whisper to the women who have come in.*) Is it Bartley it is?
ONE OF THE WOMEN:	It is surely, God rest his soul. (*Two younger women come in and pull out the table. Then men carry in the body of Bartley, laid on a plank, with a bit of a sail over it, and lay it on the table.*)
CATHLEEN:	(*To the women, as they are doing so.*) What way was he drowned?
ONE OF THE WOMEN:	The gray pony knocked him into the sea, and he was washed out where there is a great surf on the white rocks. (*Maurya has gone over and knelt down at the head of the table. The women are keening [crying] softly and swaying themselves with a slow movement. Cathleen and Nora kneel at the other end of the table. The men kneel near the door.*)
MAURYA:	(*Raising her head and speaking as if she did not see the people around her.*) They're all gone now, and there isn't anything more the sea can do to me. . . . I'll have no call now to be up crying and praying when the wind breaks from the south, and you can hear the surf is in the east, and the

surf is in the west, making a great stir with the two noises, and they hitting one on the other. I'll have no call now to be going down and getting Holy Water in the dark nights after Samhain, and I won't care what way the sea is when the other women will be keening. (*To Nora*) Give me the Holy Water, Nora, there's a small sup still on the dresser.

(*Nora gives it to her. Maurya drops Michael's clothes across Bartley's feet, and sprinkles the Holy Water over him.*)

It isn't that I haven't prayed for you, Bartley, to the Almighty God. It isn't that I haven't said prayers in the dark night till you wouldn't know what I'ld be saying; but it's a great rest I'll have now, and it's time surely. It's a great rest I'll have now, and great sleeping in the long nights after Samhain, if it's only a bit of wet flour we do have to eat, and maybe a fish that would be stinking.

(*She kneels down again, crossing herself, and saying prayers under her breath.*)

CATHLEEN: (*To an old man kneeling near her.*)

Maybe yourself and Eamon would make a coffin when the sun rises. We have fine white boards herself bought, God help her, thinking Michael would be found, and I have a new cake you can eat while you'll be working.

THE OLD MAN: (*Looking at the boards.*)

Are there nails with them?

CATHLEEN: There are not, Colum; we didn't think of the nails.

ANOTHER MAN: It's a great wonder she wouldn't think of the nails, and all the coffins she's seen made already.

CATHLEEN: It's getting old she is, and broken.

(*Maurya stands up again very slowly and spreads out the pieces of Michael's clothes beside the body, sprinkling them with the last of the Holy Water.*)

NORA: (*In a whisper to Cathleen.*)

She's quiet now and easy; but the day Michael was drowned you could hear her crying out from this to the spring well. It's fonder she was of Michael, and would any one have thought that?

CATHLEEN: (*Slowly and clearly.*)

An old woman will be soon tired with anything she will do, and isn't it nine days herself is after crying and keening, and making great sorrow in the house?

MAURYA: (*Puts the empty cup mouth downwards on the table, and lays her hands together on Bartley's feet.*)

They're all together this time, and the end is come. May the Almighty God have mercy on Bartley's soul, and on Michael's soul, and on the souls of Sheamus and Patch, and Stephen and Shawn (*Bending her head*); and may He have mercy on my soul, Nora, and on the soul of every one is left living in the world.

(*She pauses, and the keen rises a little more loudly from the women, then sinks away. Continuing.*)

Michael has a clean burial in the far north, by the grace of the Almighty God. Bartley will have a fine coffin out of the white boards, and a deep grave surely. What more can we want than that? No man at all can be living for ever, and we must be satisfied.

(*She kneels down again and the curtain falls slowly.*)

Answer **two** of the following questions. Each question is worth 15 marks.

1 What type of character do you imagine Maurya to be? Support your answer by reference to the text.

2 How is the language of the extract different from the language that we use today? Select features of the language to illustrate the differences.

3 Imagine you are the producer of this scene. It is most important to create an appropriate atmosphere and setting. Give a description of the set (props, stage layout), costumes, lighting and any other aid you would use to create this atmosphere and setting.

(2000, Paper 2, Section 1(B) Other Drama)

The final piece of unseen drama is a contemporary play but it is set in a historical period, the early nineteenth century.

D Read the episode from *Boat Memory* carefully and answer all three questions which follow.

Setting the scene

The following extract is the opening scene from the play *Boat Memory* by Laline Paull.

Boat Memory

Laline Paull

St Mary's Schoolroom Walthamstow. December 1830. There are hand-made signs from the Scriptures on walls – 'Love One Another', 'Christ Died for Our Sins', 'Fear God', etc.

Led by Hannah Bridges, the ragged little class marches round two by two, chanting the two times tables. Behind her, some of the boys bare their teeth at the girls, who get upset. Hannah stops the march.

HANNAH:	(*To the culprits*) Would you rather be out in the fields, or burnt up a flue every day, or pulling a barge in your bare bleeding feet with an empty belly? For you surely don't care to better yourself here at school, do you?
BOY:	Like you, miss?
	The class titters. Hannah points her ruler at one of the scriptural signs.
HANNAH:	What does that say?
BOY:	Dunno, miss. . .
HANNAH:	'Obey them that have rule over you.' Hebrews thirteen, seventeen. Will I tell the Reverend that you defy the Bible's authority as well as mine?
BOY:	No, miss. . .
HANNAH:	Well then. Now again, this time in threes.
GIRL:	But miss, miss, the cannibals are coming!
ANOTHER BOY:	Chew your shanks and grisly ears, yum yum.
GIRL:	My ears are not grisly –
BOY:	Slurp the marrow from your bones –
ANOTHER BOY:	Blood running everywhere –
	The boys turn on the girls, who get frightened.
HANNAH:	You will all be quite safe, anyone could see you'd taste horrid. (*The class laughs*) Do you really think the Reverend who loves us all would endanger us by bringing bloodthirsty cannibals to school here? Even if they come from . . . (*Carefully*) Tierra del Fuego, which is in South America, which is –
GIRL:	Which is where they should stay, miss, my ma says.
BOY:	And my da says school's a waste on girls and savages anyway.
GIRL:	Miss, miss, but is it true they come all the way from London in a jarvey? How many shillings is that, on savages!
HANNAH:	I do not know and I am not likely to.
BOY:	They'll eat all our food.

GIRL:	And smother us in our beds while we sleep!
	Hannah raps the ruler for order.
HANNAH:	Reverend says they are God's children in need of His Light, and we are lucky enough to be chosen to help them find it. It's a privilege!
GIRL:	But miss, miss, I'm frightened, don't make me sit next to them.
BOY:	Black devils with yellow eyes –
	The girls start crying again.
GIRL:	I'm not scared of them –
BOY:	Me neither, I'm going to bring in the pig knife and when they try to eat me I'll – and I'll – (*Mimes stabbing a girl, who starts crying*) – oh, be a cannibal properly – (*He thumps her in annoyance*)
HANNAH:	You will do no such thing! (*As chaos breaks out*) Sit down at once, all of you!
	But the game sweeps the class, the boys attacking the girls, some of whom fight back as cannibals, some cowering.
	(*Completely ignored*) Sit down!
	Behind her, Matthew Wilson enters, elegant in his public–school uniform. Seeing him, the class quickly take their places.
	I should think so too – when I give you an instruction I expect you to take it at once – Reverend Wilson has given me authority in this classroom and you will obey it. For though I be but young and a female, I can read and write as well as a man, and that is a fact.
MATTHEW:	But how is your trigonometry?
HANNAH:	Oh! Good day to you . . . Mr Wilson.
MATTHEW:	Good day to you, Hannah. Miss Bridges.
	An awkward little pause.

Questions

1 From reading this extract, what is your impression of Walthamstow school?
2 This is a humorous scene. How is the humour created?
3 Imagine you are the director of this play. Write out the text of a talk advising one of the following actors about how to perform the role in this scene:
    • Hannah
    • Boy
    • Girl
    • Matthew

STUDIED DRAMA

The second question you must answer in the Drama section is a question on a play studied by you in class. If you have seen a performance of the play either on stage or a movie of the play then you should make use of this in your answer. Knowledge of stagecraft and precise reference to specific productions of the drama merit higher marks in the exam.

You need to revise certain aspects of the drama in preparation for the exam. The types of question asked in the exam fall into the following categories:

- Discussion of a central character in the play
- Themes or issues explored by the play
- Key scenes or moments of great importance
- Directing a scene from the play
- Relationships between characters including conflict
- Dramatic development of the story leading to a climax
- Personal response to characters, scenes or themes
- The world of the play expressed through attitudes and values

This is not an exhaustive list. Certain new approaches may emerge but the key factors of good drama remain the same. If you prepare to cover a reasonable range of these questions then the options available to you in the Junior Certificate will allow you to answer this section well with this material.

In order to revise efficiently you need to identify the following:

- Your favourite character and why you like that person so much
- Your favourite moment in the story and the reason it held you attention so well
- The opening scene
- The moment of greatest dramatic tension in the play, the climax
- How the key problem or question was resolved or concluded

If you select and learn these aspects well then you will have more than enough material to deal with this section of the drama. For each scene you revise you must know what takes place, who is involved, and crucially you must learn key quotations from the text. Avoid writing a mere summary of the action of the play. Instead your answer should focus on discussing the question by making precise points, backing them up with quotations and explaining the meaning of those lines.

The following question demands that you give clear information, show that you know the text and explain your own response to the action of the scene.

1 Name a play you have studied.
2 Choose a scene from this play you found either happy **or** sad. Describe how the playwright conveys this happiness or sadness.   (30)
  (2004, Paper 1, Section 1, Drama)

SAMPLE ANSWER

My favourite scene from *Romeo and Juliet* by William Shakespeare is Act II scene 2. This scene takes place in Juliet Capulet's garden at night-time after the feast where the 'star crossed lovers' meet for the very first time. I enjoyed this scene above all others because it is the happiest scene in the play, in my opinion the hero and heroine are never quite as happy at any other point in the story.

It begins in a comical way, as Juliet is high on a balcony while Romeo is beneath her in the garden hidden from her view. Romeo is happy because he has fallen in love, again! Seeing his new love appear lit up in the window, he joyfully declares that 'Juliet is the sun'. This happy metaphor is just the first of many beautiful images in this scene. I really like the lines he says when he sees her leaning out, resting her cheek on her hand,

'O that I were a glove upon that hand,
That I might touch that cheek!'

This is a very intimate and pleasant wish and we enjoy hearing him express it because we know his wish will be granted when he embraces her later.

It is a happy scene because Juliet's wish also comes true in this scene. Unaware of the fact that she is being spied on by Romeo, she wistfully regrets that a mere name divides them from each other. Referring to Romeo as a beautiful flower she insists that 'that which we call a rose by any other word would smell as sweet'. The fact that she is unhappy thinking they will never be lovers adds to the eventual happiness of the scene since we know Romeo is about to appear and declare his love.

All the barriers between them, as members of the feuding Montague and Capulet clans, are overcome when he bravely scales the wall and climbs up to kiss her. In this scene the ridiculous proposal of marriage is a happy antidote to the vicious antagonism of the 'ancient grudge' the families bear for one another. When Romeo begs her 'Wilt thou leave me so unsatisfied', the audience shares in his delicious joy that she accepts him and the impossible dream comes true as they are engaged in spite of all the obstacles to their love.

Shakespeare realistically mixes happiness with sadness at the end of this scene because the lovers must say goodbye. Juliet expresses this perfectly when she tell him that 'parting is such sweet sorrow'. Even though he must leave we are happy in the knowledge that she will be reunited with him soon.

EXAM QUESTION D

Select one question, plan and write your answer in light of the directions given above.

1 Select a play you have studied and choose from it a scene where conflict occurs.
   (a) Outline what happens in this scene.
   (b) What are the underlying causes of the conflict in this scene?
   Support your answer by reference to the play as a whole.   (30)

OR

2 Choose your favourite character from a play you have studied.
   (a) Why do you find this character interesting? Support your answer by reference to the text.
   (b) Discuss the relationship between your chosen character and one other character in the play. Refer to the text in support of your answer.   (30)
   (2005, Paper 2, Section 1, Drama)

Remember: Your points must be supported by quotations or references to specific moments from the play and you should explain these points clearly.

Section 6 Poetry

You will answer two poetry questions in your Junior Certificate exam: the Unseen Poetry and Studied Poems. There is usually a connecting theme or idea between these questions. Developing the skill of careful reading is essential and in order to ensure this you must practice a range of Unseen Poetry questions.

UNSEEN POETRY

The first half of this section presents ten unseen poems and exercises based on typical exam questions. Spend twenty-five minutes on each question, the time available to you in the exam. A model answer is given for the first Unseen Poetry question.

A   Read the poem 'In Memory of George Best' and answer both questions.

In Memory of George Best

Dermot Bolger

In one corner of our minds it remains 1969:
Frosted pavements, icy breath, yet our hands thaw

In the thrill of chasing a ball under streetlights,
Voices in the dark calling the names of Best and Law.

A drudge of decades have clogged our arteries,
Yet no matter what occurred, what we have become,

When we see again his feint, his sheer artistry
Thousands of us are instantaneously made young.

Questions
1   What images does the poet recall from his childhood?
2   How would you describe the tone of the poem?

Answer 1

The poet remembers playing football with his friends in the streets in '1969'. The death of George Best reminds him of 'the thrill of chasing a ball under streetlights'. As a child he was inspired to play by the 'sheer artistry' of his heroes.

Another image is of the cold weather as the boys played in spite of the 'frosted pavements and icy breath' of wintertime.

Bolger also creates for us the sounds he heard as he played. He and his pals called out to each other 'the names of Best and Law' pretending to be famous soccer players.

Answer 2

The tone or feeling of this poem is nostalgic. The death of his hero, George Best, makes the poet remember the good times when he was young. When he thinks again about 'chasing a ball under streetlights' he feels happy.

The poet also feels regret that he is no longer a child enjoying the fun of a street game. Since '1969' a 'drudge of decades' has passed and his life is not as exciting as it used to be.

I think he feels surprised that his hero's 'sheer artistry' can work like magic on so many people who are 'instantaneously made young'. Bolger is sad that George Best is dead, but grateful that this footballer brought him so much pleasure in his life.

B   The poem 'Born Yesterday' was written by Philip Larkin to celebrate the birth of his best friend's daughter, Sally. Read the poem carefully and answer both questions. You should support the points you make with quotations from the poem.

Born Yesterday

for Sally Amis

Philip Larkin

Tightly-folded bud,
I have wished you something
None of the others would:
Not the usual stuff
About being beautiful,
Or running off a spring
Of innocence and love –
They will all wish you that,

And should it prove possible,
Well, you're a lucky girl.
But if it shouldn't, then
May you be ordinary;
Have, like other women,
An average of talents:
Not ugly, not good-looking,
Nothing uncustomary
To pull you off balance,
That, unworkable itself,
Stops all the rest from working.
In fact, may you be dull –
If that is what a skilled,
Vigilant, flexible,
Unemphasised, enthralled
Catching of happiness is called.

Questions

1   What are the poet's wishes for the girl as she grows up?
2   If you were one of the baby's parents would you be pleased with this poem?
    Explain your answer.
3   Do you think that this is a well-written poem?
    Defend your point of view with reference to the text of the poem.

HINTS FOR APPROACHING UNSEEN QUESTIONS

1   The first question about the poem 'Born Yesterday' asks about the poet's (Philip Larkin) wishes for the new baby girl. This implies that he has several wishes or hopes for the child as she gets older. In the first stanza he uses the verb 'wish' twice. Look closely at what he is saying here.

You may also notice that the poet contrasts his own hopes for Sally with the wishes of 'all the others'. Clearly he feels that his vision of her future is unconventional in some way. A further clue in the second stanza is when he says 'May you be . . . .' Here he is clearly telling us what he hopes will happen as she matures.

The remainder of the poem is a development or explanation of this wish as he clarifies what he means in a list of certain qualities. These adjectives really give the strongest idea of the kind of person the poet hopes Sally will become.

2   The second question requires you to show that you know what the poet hopes for the child. Once you identify again the essential detail of his ambition for her, you are free to argue either that you would be happy or unhappy with the poet's wish. The essential thing is to explain why you would be pleased or displeased and refer to words or phrases from the poem in writing your answer.

3   The final question relating to 'Born Yesterday' is typical of recent exam questions and does require you to have a clear idea of what it is that makes a poem work.

A really good poem will evoke a strong feeling in the reader. Does the poem make you react in any way? If you do have a clear response then you may argue that the poem is well written because it has a definite emotional effect on you. Show how this happens by quoting the precise words and explaining your reaction to them.

Imagery or sound effects can also contribute to the overall impact a poem makes. You might say that the poem is good because a particular image is compelling, or because of the effect of rhyme or alliteration.

Another option is to say how the poem makes you think about life in a new or interesting way. The best poetry challenges our beliefs about ourselves and the world around us.

C Read the poem 'Fireworks' and answer all three questions. Your answer should refer to words or phrases in the poem to support the points you make.

Fireworks

James Reeves

They rise like sudden fiery flowers
That burst upon the night,
Then fall to earth in burning showers
Of crimson, blue and white.

Like buds too wonderful to name,
Each miracle unfolds
And Catherine wheels begin to flame
Like whirling marigolds.

Rockets and Roman candles make
An orchard of the sky,
Where magic trees their petals shake
Upon each gazing eye.

Questions

1 Choose any interesting metaphor in the poem and say why you like it.
2 How does the writer evoke sound in the poem?
3 Describe the atmosphere or mood created in this poem.

D   Read Gillian Clarke's poem 'Miracle on St David's Day' and answer two of the three
    questions below.

Miracle on St David's Day
Gillian Clarke

'They flash upon that inward eye
Which is the bliss of solitude'
The Daffodils by W. Wordsworth.

An afternoon yellow and open-mouthed
with daffodils. The sun treads the path
among cedars and enormous oaks.
It might be a country house, guests strolling,
the rumps of gardeners between nursery shrubs.

I am reading poetry to the insane.
An old woman, interrupting, offers
as many buckets of coal as I need.
A beautiful chestnut-haired boy listens
entirely absorbed. A schizophrenic ...

on a good day, they tell me later.
In a cage of first March sun, a woman
sits not listening, not seeing, not feeling.
In her neat clothes the woman is absent.
A big, mild man is tenderly led

to his chair. He has never spoken.
His labourer's hands on his knees, he rocks
gently to the rhythms of the poems.
I read to their presences, absences,
to the big, dumb labouring man as he rocks.

He is suddenly standing, silently,
huge and mild, but I feel afraid. Like slow
movement of spring water or the first bird

of the year in the breaking darkness,
the labourer's voice recites, "The Daffodils"…

The nurses are frozen, alert; the patients
seem to listen. He is hoarse but word-perfect.
Outside the daffodils are still as wax,
a thousand, ten thousand, their syllables
unspoken, their creams and yellows still.

Forty years ago, in a Valleys school,
the class recited poetry by rote.
Since the dumbness of misery fell
he has remembered there was a music
of speech and that once he had something to say.

When he's done, before the applause, we observe
the flowers' silence. A thrush sings
and the daffodils are flame.

Questions
1   What is the miracle to which the title refers?
2   The poet reads for an unusual audience. Describe her audience in this poem.
3   What does the poet reveal about the power of our imagination?

E   Read the poem 'Carentan O Carentan' and then answer the questions which follow.

Carentan O Carentan

Louis Simpson

Trees in the old days used to stand
And shape a shady lane
Where lovers wandered hand in hand
Who came from Carentan.

This was the shining green canal
Where we came two by two

Walking at combat-interval.
Such trees we never knew.

The day was early June, the ground
Was soft and bright with dew.
Far away the guns did sound,
But here the sky was blue.

The sky was blue, but there a smoke
Hung still above the sea
Where the ships together spoke
To towns we could not see.

Could you have seen us through a glass
You would have said a walk
Of farmers out to turn the grass.
Each with his own hay-fork.

The watchers in their leopard suits
Waited till it was time,
And aimed between the belt and boot
And let the barrel climb.

I must lie down at once, there is
A hammer at my knee.
And call it death or cowardice,
Don't count again on me.

Everything's all right, Mother,
Everyone gets the same
At one time or another.
It's all in the game.

I never strolled, nor ever shall,
Down such a leafy lane.
I never drank in a canal,
Nor ever shall again.

There is a whistling in the leaves
And it is not the wind,
The twigs are falling from the knives
That cut men to the ground.

Tell me, Master-Sergeant,
The way to turn and shoot.
But the Sergeant's silent
That taught me how to do it.

Captain, show us quickly
Our place upon the map.
But the Captain's sickly
And taking a long nap.

Lieutenant, what's my duty,
My place in the platoon?
He too's a sleeping beauty,
Charmed by that strange tune.

Carentan O Carentan
Before we met with you
We never yet had lost a man
Or knew what death could do.

1   There are many contrasting images in the poem. What is the effect of these contrasts?
2   How does the speaker feel about the town of Carentan?
3   Suggest an alternative title for this poem and explain your title with detailed reference to the text of the poem.

F.   Read the poem 'Watching Walls' and answer the questions which follow.

Watching Walls

Mary O'Gorman

Pull yourself together; he implores
I watch walls edge across black floors.

Don't turn back now daughters protest
Their incline is my Everest.

Pick up that phone, my close friends coax
As they make tea, make sense, make jokes.

Let's try new pills, the doctor sighs,
I stare at the spiders in his eyes.

Please try to sleep, a ward nurse begs,
There's a cobwebbed Christ on the window ledge.

How did this happen, my dead mother asks
Tormented butterflies batter the glass.

Questions
1   How does the poet convey the pain of depression in this poem?
2   Which image do you find most effective? Explain your choice.
3   What feelings does the poem create in you?

G   Read the poem 'Coming' and answer the questions which follow.

Coming

Philip Larkin

On longer evenings,
Light, chill and yellow,
Bathes the serene
Foreheads of houses.
A thrush sings,
Laurel-surrounded
In the deep bare garden,
Its fresh-peeled voice
Astonishing the brickwork.
It will be spring soon,
It will be spring soon –
And I, whose childhood
Is a forgotten boredom,
Feel like a child
Who comes on a scene
Of adult reconciling,
And can understand nothing
But the unusual laughter,
And starts to be happy.

Questions

1   What alerts the poet to the approach of spring?
2   How does he explain his feelings about the arrival of the new season?
3   Do you think Philip Larkin is a poet you would like to read more of? Based on
    the evidence from this poem give reasons for your answer.

H   Read the poem 'The Charge of the Light Brigade' and answer any two of the
    questions which follow.

The Charge of the Light Brigade
Alfred, Lord Tennyson

Half a league, half a league,
Half a league onward,
All in the valley of Death
Rode the six hundred.
'Forward, the Light Brigade!
Charge for the guns!' he said:
Into the valley of Death
Rode the six hundred.

'Forward, the Light Brigade!'
Was there a man dismay'd?
Not tho' the soldier knew
Someone had blunder'd:
Theirs not to make reply,
Theirs not to reason why,
Theirs but to do and die:
Into the valley of Death
Rode the six hundred.

Cannon to right of them,
Cannon to left of them,
Cannon in front of them
Volley'd and thunder'd;
Storm'd at with shot and shell,
Boldly they rode and well,
Into the jaws of Death,
Into the mouth of Hell
Rode the six hundred.

Flash'd all their sabres bare,

Flash'd as they turn'd in air,
Sabring the gunners there,
Charging an army, while
All the world wonder'd:
Plunged in the battery-smoke
Right thro' the line they broke;
Cossack and Russian
Reel'd from the sabre stroke
Shatter'd and sunder'd.
Then they rode back, but not
Not the six hundred.

Cannon to right of them,
Cannon to left of them,
Cannon behind them
Volley'd and thunder'd;
Storm'd at with shot and shell,
While horse and hero fell,
They that had fought so well
Came thro' the jaws of Death
Back from the mouth of Hell,
All that was left of them,
Left of six hundred.

When can their glory fade?
O the wild charge they made!
All the world wonder'd.
Honor the charge they made,
Honor the Light Brigade,
Noble six hundred.

Questions
1   What is the attitude of the soldiers as they charge?
2   Comment on the poet's use of rhythm, rhyme and repetition.
3   Choose an image from the poem which you found striking and say why
    it is effective.

I   Read the poem 'Leaning into the afternoons . . .' by Pablo Neruda and answer the
    questions which follow.

Leaning into the afternoons . . .
Pablo Neruda

Leaning into the afternoons I cast my sad nets
towards your oceanic eyes.

There in the highest blaze my solitude lengthens and flames,
its arms turning like a drowning man's.

I send out red signals across your absent eyes
that wave like the sea or the beach by a lighthouse.

You keep only darkness, my distant female,
from your regard sometimes the coast of dread emerges.

Leaning into the afternoons I fling my sad nets
to that sea that is thrashed by your oceanic eyes.

The birds of night peck at the first stars
that flash like my soul when I love you.

The night gallops on its shadowy mare
shedding blue tassels over the land.

Questions
1   The speaker in this love poem is a fisherman. How does he make use of his
    knowledge of the sea in expressing his love?
2   Describe the woman he addresses in this poem.
3   Do you think this is a good love poem? Give reasons for your answer based on
    evidence from the poem.

J   Read the poem 'My Room' and answer the questions which follow.

My Room
Patrick Kavanagh

10 by 12
And a low roof,
If I stand by the side wall
My head feels the reproof.

Five holy pictures
Hang on the walls –
The Virgin and Child,
St Anthony of Padua,
St Patrick our own,
Leo XIII
And the Little Flower.

My bed in the centre,
So many things to me –
A dining table,
A writing desk,
A couch,
And a slumber palace.

My room is a musty attic,
But its little window
Lets in the stars.

Questions
1   What does his description of the room tell us about Patrick Kavanagh?
2   What is your understanding of the last two lines?
    'But its little window
    Lets in the stars'
3   Do you like or dislike this poem? Give reasons for your answer based on evidence
    from the poem.

STUDIED POETRY

In the course of your three years as a Junior Certificate student you have read many poems. The Studied Poetry question tests your understanding of the poems you have explored in class. You must select a group of up to ten poems in order to be able to answer the range of possible questions in this section. The poems you choose should be selected based on your answers to the following questions.

1   Name the poem you like the best and the poem you like the least. Explain by comparing the two, why you liked one and disliked the other.
2   Name two poems, written by different poets, dealing with a similar theme.
3   Identify a poet whose work you enjoyed and give the titles of two poems you studied by that poet.
4   Select two poems you studied which contain curious or interesting images.
5   Find two poems where the poet made clever use of the sound of words in the poem.
6   Choose two poems which arouse intense feelings in you.

In choosing poems you should find some poems will satisfy more than one of the criteria above. For example, of the unseen poems in this chapter two poems on a theme of war are 'Carentan O Carentan' and 'The Charge of the Light Brigade'. Both poems also contain interesting images and the second makes clever use of the sound of words. You might also include the two poems by the poet Philip Larkin and select 'Born Yesterday' as you favourite poem. 'Coming' deals with the subject of nature and has several examples of powerful metaphors.

A good selection of poems will include enough to cover the range of possible questions outlined above.

You should know the title of the poem, the name of the poet and a number of useful quotations. The Poetry question requires you to examine the poem carefully and focus your answer on the questions asked of you. It is vital to support your answer with precise and accurate quotations from the poem. Some of your poems will be short and easier to learn because of the poet's use of rhyme, rhythm and other sound effects.

Above all, you must give some thought to the reasons for choosing certain poems. Many poetry questions have required students to give their own individual response to a favourite poem or to show how a poem helped you to make sense of some area of your own life. For this reason, you must be able to say why you have chosen certain poems.

It is also important to know the meaning of some of the words used when discussing poetry. A brief glossary of these terms is given in Section 2 of this book under the heading 'Figures of Speech' (p. 38).

Answer either 1 or 2 which follow.

1   From the poetry studied by you choose a poem which is set in an interesting time or place.
    (a) Describe the setting.
    (b) What does this setting contribute to the effectiveness of the poem? Give reasons for your answer based on evidence from the poem.   (30)

OR

2   From the poetry you have studied choose a poem which deals with either youth or old age.
    (a) What pictures does this poem give of either youth or old age?
    (b) What is your personal response to the picture of youth or old age given in the poem? Support your answer with reference to the poem.   (30)
    (2005, Paper 2, Section 2, Poetry)

SAMPLE ANSWERS

Answer 1(a)

A poem I studied called 'Carentan O Carentan' is set in an interesting time and place. The location is also the name of the poem, Carentan is a town or village described by the poet in great detail. Louis Simpson tells us about the 'shady lane where lovers wandered' and of the 'shining green canal' that flows through the town. This pleasant scene takes place in 'early June', probably in the morning as the 'ground was soft and bright with dew'. The trees, the canal, and the soft, bright dew give us an impression of a tranquil pastoral setting.

We discover, however, that there is something sinister about this location at this precise moment. The speaker and his friends are being observed by 'watchers in their leopard suits' and this illusion of peace is about to be torn apart. Carentan is now the location for an ambush. In contrast to the earlier picture of calm beauty is the scene of carnage, the 'whistling in the leaves' is 'not the wind' but a hail of gunfire. The setting therefore is both beautiful and horrific. Carentan is remembered not only for its picturesque charm but also as a war zone and the scene of a massacre.

Answer 1(b)

The initial setting of tranquil beauty creates a relaxed mood in the poem 'Carentan O Carentan'. 'The sky was blue' and the poet tells us the men looked like a group of 'farmers out to turn the grass'. In a scene like this we expect something pleasant to happen. The poet even refers to Carentan as a place where 'lovers wandered hand in hand'. Instead of love or beauty the scene becomes one of horror and violence.

The contrast between the two scenes makes the poem very dramatic. We are surprised by the ferocious attack 'that cut men to the ground'. Instead of a relaxing stroll the journey is a fatal walk into the jaws of a trap. I think this is very effective because the stark change emphasises how awful the ambush must have been. Also, just like the soldiers, we the readers are taken by surprise. The sudden change is shocking for us in a similar way to the surprise felt by the soldiers.

This is a very effective and memorable war poem because it focuses on a specific time and place. It is not a poem I enjoyed reading but the 'shady lane', 'shining canal' and 'blue' sky give me a clear picture of the place before the battle happens.

Section 7 Fiction

The Fiction section is Section 3 of Paper 2. You must answer an Unseen Fiction question and a Studied Fiction section. These carry equal marks.

Essentially you must apply the same skills of close reading tested in the Reading question of Paper 1 to the Unseen Fiction question. Marks are awarded for relevant points supported by references to the text and clearly explained. As with the earlier questions you should read the story, highlighting key points. When you read the question, identify the key words and highlight them. You will find material useful for your answer in the area of the text where you can locate these key words.

Aim to make a variety of points for each answer and try to link or connect these points.

Your time is quite limited so be careful to divide the time available between all parts of the question. Once the time for a question is up, move on to the next one.

UNSEEN FICTION

All fiction involves storytelling. Sometimes there will be a narrator or storyteller who can be easily identified. If the character is telling his or her own story then it is a first-person narrator. If the character is referred to as 'he' or 'she', 'him' or 'her' then it is a third person narrator. Occasionally a question will focus on the person telling the story, asking you to deal with the narrator's attitudes or feelings about another character or some aspect of the plot.

PLOT

Many Fiction questions will require you to explain details of the plot or storyline in the narrative. You may be asked to clarify a sequence of events, the causes of an incident or the consequences of certain actions. Here it is important to logically outline the connection between events in a coherent way.

CHARACTERS

The second most relevant aspect of fiction is character. Most Unseen Fiction questions will include a task related to the characters in the story. You might be asked to examine the nature of a character, his or her behaviour and outlook. On the other hand these questions often centre on the relationship between characters, possibly some form of conflict, or even a simple contrast in the actions and attitudes of characters in a narrative text.

STYLE

A slightly more complex task is a question related to the writer's technique. Sometimes you will be asked to dwell on the author's style, the overall tone or atmosphere of a story and the way the writer achieves this effect. In questions of style your answer must concentrate on the words and phrases used in the passage in order to give support to your views.

PROSE FICTION

Finally you may be asked for your response to a piece of prose fiction. Here the emphasis is on you as a young reader. You should always be aware of the feelings and ideas the story evokes in you. Your judgement of the quality of a story is influenced by other novels and stories you have read in the past. Before the exam you must give some thought to the types of story you enjoy and ask yourself why you like these stories. Perhaps you enjoy romances, thrillers or fantasy adventures. Your knowledge and experience as a reader is very relevant to the answers you write in this section of the exam. It is useful to be able to say what type of stories you prefer and why you enjoy them.

What follows are a number of Unseen Fiction questions and one sample answer.

A   Read the story below and answer all four questions which follow. The story is by Patricia Lynch and is called *The Dragon Ring of Connla*.

The Dragon Ring of Connla
Patricia Lynch

Cuchulain had only one son and, after he had finished his own training with Scatha in the Land of Shadows, he left a ring for the child and asked that he should be called Connla.

'Train him as you trained me,' he said. 'When he has grown big enough for it to fit his finger, give him the ring. And let him be under *geis* (bond) not to make himself known, never to turn out of the way for any man and never to refuse a fight!'

Years later, when Cuchulain had become a great champion, King Conor of Ulster and some of his warriors were gathered on the shore, when they saw a boat coming over the sea.

'That's a strange boat!' exclaimed Conor. 'Can it be made of bronze?'

Sunlight gleamed on the boat, on the golden oars and on the fair hair of the boy who rode towards them. Presently he pulled in the oars and, while the boat drifted landwards on the tide, he took up his sling, chose a stone from a heap lying before him and cast at a sea bird flying overhead, so that it fell alive at his feet.

'I wonder where that lad comes from!' muttered Conor.

'If he can fight as well as he casts, the men of his country must be great warriors. If they invaded Ulster, we'd be destroyed. Go down Condery; warn him to keep away.'

As the boat drew in, Condery strode to the edge of the sea and shouted to the stranger not to come ashore.

'I'm going to land at this very spot!' declared the boy. 'I'll not turn back for you or anyone!'

He leaped from the boat, thrust it off with his spear and splashed up the strand.

Conall of the Victories, amazed that Condery had allowed the boy to leave the boat, marched down to them. Before he came within speaking distance, the young stranger picked up the largest stone he could see and hurled it at the warrior. Conall fell senseless and, while he lay unconscious, the boy ran over to him and bound his arms.

Condery, who was unarmed, retreated and another warrior went to subdue the young hero, but he was no luckier than Conall.

King Conor was angry. He strode to a rocky ledge above the strand and hailed the boy.

'What is your name, who is your father and where do you come from?'

'I'll not tell you!' shouted the lad. 'And I'll not go from this place if you bring your whole army against me.'

The warriors had begun by laughing at his boastfulness. Now, as Ulsterman after Ulsterman was attacked and beaten, shame made Conor furious.

'Go to Cuchulain!' he said, 'and tell him to come down to the strand and fight with the stranger, who is defeating all our warriors, even Conall of the Victories.'

Cuchulain was at home in Dundalk with Emer his wife, when the messenger came.

'Conor has a whole army, yet he must send for you!' she cried indignantly.

But Cuchulain was hanging his shield over his arm and taking down his sword and spear.

'If Conor sends for me, I'd be disgraced for ever if I didn't go!' he declared.

Emer knew that and was proud of him. But she was troubled and there was no smile on her face as he leaped into his chariot.

Cuchulain drove to where Conor and his men watched the fair boy tossing javelins into the air and catching them in order, one by one while, on the sand, lay a row of bound warriors, helpless and ashamed.

'Do you ask me to fight a boy?' Cuchulain asked Conor.

'I do!' replied the king. 'But I would sooner have him among my own warriors. Go against him, for there lies Conall of the Victories and six more of our best fighters, bound at the mercy of this young barbarian!'

'This is strange!' said Cuchulain. 'There is no boy of his age or size in Ireland could put Conall on his back. I must know more of this lad.'

He went along the strand and the boy smiled at him, still tossing his weapons and catching them easily.

'What is your name, my lad?' asked Cuchulain, 'and where do you come from?'

'I can't tell you that!' replied the boy.

'A pity!' said Cuchulain. 'For then you must die.'

'If I die, I die!' declared the strange lad.

He flung down his javelins and taking his sword, went to meet Cuchulain.

The champion did not fight seriously, for he was determined not to harm the boy. But when a lock of his hair was shorn off, he knew he must treat his opponent as a real warrior.

'We'll have no more play!' he thought.

Cuchulain was using all his strength and skill, yet he could not drive that boy back one inch. He planted himself upon a rock and stood so firmly his feet sank into the stone and, to this day, that place is called 'the strand of the footprints'.

The boy was growing tired but, with a swift turn, he gripped Cuchulain by the arm. As the Champion tried to free himself, they both toppled into the sea. Cuchulain was underneath and was drowning when he remembered the Gae Bolg. He had brought the terrible body spear with him, though he had not dreamed he would need to use it. Now he thrust it at the boy and the barbs pierced his limbs.

'I am hurt!' he cried. 'Why didn't Scatha teach me that?'

Cuchulain dragged him from the water and stretched him on the sand. The setting sun struck a flash from a ring on the boy's finger – a ring in the form of a dragon with emerald eyes, biting its own tail. Cuchulain knew the ring. He lifted the lad in his arms and laid him before Conor and the warriors.

'Here is my only son, Connla, that I have killed for you, men of Ulster!' he said.

'It is true, I am Connla!' agreed the boy. 'If only I had a few years to train among you, Cuchulain and I would have led you against the world. I thought I had years before me, but as my death has come, show me the famous warriors and let me say goodbye to them.'

Conall of the Victories, who had been set free, and the other famous men knelt and kissed him while Cuchulain stood weeping.

Then Connla died and over his grave they carved a pillar stone with the story of his short life. He was the only son Cuchulain ever had and he killed him for the honour of Ulster.

Questions
1 What is ironic about Cuchulain's instructions to Scatha?
2 This is an old Irish legend. Identify and comment on the characteristics of this style of storytelling.
3 Which character in the story do you sympathise with most?

Sample answers

Answer 1

First of all Cuchulain leaves a ring with Scatha to be given to his child. He also asks for the boy to be named 'Connla'. The 'ring in the shape of the dragon' was later one of the clues that revealed the boy's identity to his father.

It is deeply ironic that having named his own child Cuchulain is forced to ask him

'What is your name, my lad?' Of course this would never have happened if Cuchulain had not told Scatha to put Connla under '*geis* (bond) not to make himself known'. Clearly he felt it was necessary to give the boy a degree of anonymity growing up as son of the champion of Ulster. If he had known the boy's name he would not have fought him.

The instruction 'never to turn out of the way for any man' was another mistake because the boy obediently refused to submit to any of King Conor's men. If he had not been instructed to be so uncompromising then the tragic death of the boy could have been avoided. Ironically his own father helped to bring this about.

Cuchulain's final ironic request was to teach his son 'never to refuse a fight'. This was the last straw in the boy's defeat as he was under obligation to fight his own father because he was expected to bravely confront any enemy.

Answer 2

The story begins in 'the Land of Shadows'. Myths or legends are often set in a distant time or place. The names of the characters, 'Scatha', 'King Conor' and 'Conall of the Victories', are not like ordinary modern names as they imply mystery, royalty and heroism in battle.

Another feature of legends is characters with superhuman power. Connla, while still a mere boy, can fight and defeat a host of grown warriors who have already proven themselves in battle. His father has the power of a superhero too since he gains victory over Connla using the 'Gae Bolg'. This 'terrible body spear' is not a normal weapon but clearly has some magical power.

Legends usually involve heroic acts of bravery, pitched battles and tragic death. There are several examples of courage from Condrey to Cuchulain and Connla himself. The scene on the strand that day must have looked like a battle as the beach was covered with warriors 'bound at the mercy of this young barbarian'. Sadly the story includes a shocking death as Connla is killed by his own father.

One last detail that is common to myths and legends is the explanation of the name 'the strand of the footprints'. In the midst of the story we learn that the beach got its name from the marks of Cuchulain's feet left on a rock during his struggle with Connla.

Answer 3

I sympathise most with Connla in this story. He is the only one to loose his life; all of the other characters survive even though some of them have been beaten, humiliated or wounded.

He also deserves sympathy because he was killed by a member of his own family. Usually your family protect you, but because of the strange circumstances the opposite happens in this legend.

I feel sorrow for the boy because in trying to please his father by obeying his orders he unwittingly brings about his own death. It must have been hard not to divulge his true identity and then to have to do battle with his own father.

A sad aspect of Connla's life is the fact that he grew up with Scatha and not with his family. I think Connla deserves to be pitied for all these reasons.

B Read the following short story and answer the questions which follow. The story is by Bryan MacMahon and is called 'The Ring'.

The Ring

Bryan MacMahon

I should like you to have known my grandmother. She was my mother's mother, and as I remember her she was a widow with a warm farm in the Kickham country in Tipperary. Her land was on the southern slope of a hill, and there it drank in the sun which, to me, seemed always to be balanced on the teeth of the Galtees. Each year I spent the greater part of my summer holidays at my grandmother's place. It was a great change for me to leave our home in a bitter sea-coast village in Kerry and visit my grandmother's. Why, man, the grass gone to waste on a hundred yards on the roadside in Tipperary was as much as you'd find in a dozen of our sea-poisoned fields. I always thought it a pity to see all that fine grass go to waste by the verge of the road. I think so still.

Although my Uncle Con was married, my grandmother held the whip hand in the farm. At the particular time I am trying to recall, the first child was in the cradle. (Ah, how time has galloped away! That child is now a nun in a convent on the Seychelles Islands.) My Uncle Con's wife, my Aunt Annie, was a gentle, delicate girl who was only charmed in herself to have somebody to assume the responsibility of the place. Which was just as well indeed, considering the nature of woman my grandmother was. Since that time when her husband's horse had walked into the farmyard unguided, with my grandfather, Martin Dermody, dead in the body of the car, her heart had turned to stone in her breast. Small wonder to that turning, since she was left with six young children – five girls and one boy, my Uncle Con. But she faced the world bravely and did well by them all. Ah! But she was hard, main hard.

Once at a race-meeting I picked up a jockey's crop. When I balanced it on my palm it reminded me of my grandmother. Once I had a twenty-two pound salmon laced to sixteen feet of Castleconnell greenheart; the rod reminded me of my grandmother. True, like crop and rod, she had an element of flexibility, but like them there was no trace of fragility. Now after all those years I cannot recall her person clearly; to me she is but something tall and dark and austere. But lately I see things that puzzled me when I was a boy. Towards me she displayed a certain black affection. Oh, but I made her laugh warmly once. That was when I told her of the man who had stopped me on the road beyond the limekiln and asked me if I were a grandson of Martin Dermody. Inflating with a shy pride, I had told him that I was. He then gave me a shilling and said, 'Maybe you're called Martin after your grandfather?' 'No,' I said, 'I'm called Con after my Uncle Con.' It was then my grandmother had laughed a little warmly. But my Uncle Con caught me under the armpits, tousled my hair and said I was a clever Kerry rascal.

The solitary occasion on which I remember her to have shown emotion was remarkable. Maybe remarkable isn't the proper word; obscene would be closer to the mark. Obscene I would have thought of it then, had I known the meaning of the word. Today I think it merely pathetic.

How was it that it all started? Yes, there was I with my bare legs trailing from the heel of a loaded hay-float. I was watching the broad silver parallels we were leaving in the clean after-grass. My Uncle Con was standing in the front of the float guiding the mare. Drawing in the hay to the hayshed we were. Already we had a pillar and a half of the hayshed filled. My grandmother was up on the hay, forking the lighter trusses. The servant-boy was handling the heavier forkfuls. A neighbour was throwing it up to them.

When the float stopped at the hayshed I noticed that something was amiss. For one thing the man on the hay was idle, as indeed was the man on the ground. My grandmother was on the ground, looking at the hay with cold calculating eyes. She turned to my Uncle Con.

'Draw in no more hay, Con,' she said. 'I've lost my wedding ring.'

'Where? In the hay?' he queried.

'Yes, in the hay.'

'But I thought you had a keeper?'

'I've lost the keeper too. My hands are getting thin.'

'The story could be worse,' he commented.

My grandmother did not reply for a little while. She was eyeing the stack with enmity. ''Tis in that half-pillar,' she said at last. 'I must look for it.'

'You've a job before you, mother,' said Uncle Con.

She spoke to the servant-boy and the neighbour. 'Go down and shake out those couple of pikes at the end of the Bog Meadow,' she ordered. 'They're heating in the centre.'

'Can't we be drawing in to the idle pillar, mother?' my Uncle Con asked gently.

'No, Con,' she answered. 'I'll be putting the hay from the middle pillar there.'

The drawing-in was over for the day. That was about four o'clock in the afternoon. Before she tackled the half-pillar my grandmother went down on her hands and knees and started to search the loose hay in the idle pillar. She searched wisp by wisp, even sop by sop. My Uncle Con beckoned to me to come away. Anyway, we knew she'd stop at six o'clock. 'Six to six' was her motto for working hours. She never broke that rule.

That was a Monday evening. On Tuesday we offered to help – my Uncle Con and I. She was down on her hands and knees when we asked her. 'No, no,' she said abruptly. Then, by way of explanation, when she saw that we were crestfallen: 'You see, if we didn't find it I'd be worried that ye didn't search as carefully as ye should, and I'd have no peace of mind until I had searched it all over again.' So she worked hard all day, breaking off only for her meals and stopping sharp at six o'clock.

By Wednesday evening she had made a fair gap in the hay but had found no ring. Now and again during the day we used to go down to see if she had had any success. She was very wan in the face when she stopped in the evening.

On Thursday morning her face was still more strained and drawn. She seemed reluctant to leave the rick even to take her meals. What little she ate seemed like so much dust in her mouth. We took down tea to her several times during the day.

By Friday the house was on edge. My Uncle Con spoke guardedly to her at dinner-time. 'This will set us back a graydle, mother,' he said. 'I know, son: I know, son: I know,' was all she said in reply.

Saturday came and the strain was unendurable. About three o'clock in the afternoon she found the keeper. We had been watching her in turns from the kitchen window. I remember my uncle's face lighting up and his saying, 'Glory, she's found it!' But he drew a long breath when again she started burrowing feverishly in the hay. Then we knew it was only the keeper. We didn't run out at all. We waited till she came in at six o'clock. There were times between three and six when our three heads were together at the small window watching her. I was thinking she was like a mouse nibbling at a giant's loaf.

At six she came in and said, 'I found the keeper.' After her tea she couldn't stay still. She fidgeted around the kitchen for an hour or so. Then, 'Laws were made to be broken,' said my grandmother with brittle bravery, and she stalked out to the hayshed. Again we watched her.

Coming on for dusk she returned and lighted a stable lantern and went back to resume her search. Nobody crossed her. We didn't say yes aye or no to her. After a time my Uncle Con took her heavy coat off the rack and went down and threw it across her shoulders. I was with him. 'There's a touch of frost here tonight, mother,' said my Uncle Con.

We loitered for a while in the darkness outside the ring of her lantern's light. But she resented our pitying eyes so we went in. We sat around the big fire waiting – Uncle Con, Aunt Annie and I. That was the lonely waiting – without speaking – just as if we were waiting for an old person to die or for a child to come into the world. Near twelve we heard her step on the cobbles. 'Twas typical of my grandmother that she placed the lantern on the ledge of the dresser and quenched the candle in it before she spoke to us.

'I found it,' she said. The words dropped out of her drawn face.

'Get hot milk for my mother, Annie,' said Uncle Con briskly.

My grandmother sat by the fire, a little to one side. Her face was as cold as death. I kept watching her like a hawk but her eyes didn't even flicker. The wedding ring was inside its keeper, and my grandmother kept twirling it round and round with the fingers of her right hand.

Suddenly, as if ashamed of her fingers' betrayal, she hid her hands under her check apron. Then, unpredictably, the fists under the apron came up to meet her face, and her face bent down to meet the fists in the apron. 'Oh, Martin, Martin,' she sobbed, and then she cried like the rain.

Questions

1   What sort of person was the storyteller's grandmother?
2   Why do you think this particular memory stands out in his mind?
3   How does the writer create a tense feeling in this short story?
4   Do you find the language and imagery of this story appealing in any way? Explain your answer.

C   Read the following extract and answer the questions which follow. The extract is taken from the novel *Jane Eyre* by Charlotte Brontë.

Background to the novel

In the novel *Jane Eyre*, the eponymous heroine, Jane, is an orphan who escapes her cruel Aunt Reed only to suffer further hardship at the Lowood Institution, a home for orphaned children. Here she meets a kind mentor Miss Temple and befriends another girl called Helen Burns. In the extract below Jane leaves her own dormitory late at night to visit her sick friend who is being treated for a serious illness and kept in isolation in Miss Temple's room.

Jane Eyre
Charlotte Brontë

It might be two hours later, probably near eleven, when I – not having been able to fall asleep, and deeming, from the perfect silence of the dormitory, that my companions were all wrapt in profound repose – rose softly, put on my frock over my night-dress, and, without shoes, crept from the apartment, and set off in quest of Miss Temple's room. It was quite at the other end of the house; but I knew my way; and the light of the unclouded summer moon, entering here and there at passage windows, enabled me to find it without difficulty. An odour of camphor and burnt vinegar warned me when I came near the fever room: and I passed its door quickly, fearful lest the nurse who sat up all night should hear me. I dreaded being discovered and sent back; for I must see Helen, – I must embrace her before she died, – I must give her one last kiss, exchange with her one last word.

Having descended a staircase, traversed a portion of the house below, and succeeded in opening and shutting, without noise, two doors, I reached another flight of steps; these I mounted, and then just opposite to me was Miss Temple's room. A light shone through the keyhole and from under the door; a profound stillness pervaded the vicinity. Coming near, I found the door slightly ajar; probably to admit some fresh air into the close abode of sickness. Indisposed to hesitate, and full of impatient impulses – soul and senses quivering with keen throes – I put it back and looked in. My eye sought Helen, and feared to find death.

Close by Miss Temple's bed, and half covered with its white curtains, there stood a little crib. I saw the outline of a form under the clothes, but the face was hid by the hangings: the nurse I had spoken to in the garden sat in an easy-chair asleep; an unsnuffed candle burnt dimly on the table. Miss Temple was not to be seen: I knew afterwards that she had been called to a delirious patient in the fever-room. I advanced; then paused by the crib side: my hand was on the curtain, but I preferred speaking before I withdrew it. I still recoiled at the dread of seeing a corpse.

'Helen!' I whispered softly, 'are you awake?'

She stirred herself, put back the curtain, and I saw her face, pale, wasted, but quite composed: she looked so little changed that my fear was instantly dissipated.

'Can it be you, Jane?' she asked, in her own gentle voice.

'Oh!' I thought, 'she is not going to die; they are mistaken: she could not speak and look so calmly if she were.'

I got on to her crib and kissed her: her forehead was cold, and her cheek both cold and thin, and so were her hand and wrist; but she smiled as of old.

'Why are you come here, Jane? It is past eleven o'clock: I heard it strike some minutes since.'

'I came to see you, Helen: I heard you were very ill, and I could not sleep till I had spoken to you.'

'You came to bid me good-bye, then: you are just in time probably.'

'Are you going somewhere, Helen? Are you going home?'

'Yes; to my long home – my last home.'

'No, no, Helen!' I stopped, distressed. While I tried to devour my tears, a fit of coughing seized Helen; it did not, however, wake the nurse; when it was over, she lay some minutes exhausted; then she whispered –

'Jane, your little feet are bare; lie down and cover yourself with my quilt.'

I did so: she put her arm over me, and I nestled close to her. After a long silence, she resumed, still whispering –

'I am very happy, Jane; and when you hear that I am dead, you must be sure and not grieve: there is nothing to grieve about. We all must die one day, and the illness which is removing me is not painful; it is gentle and gradual: my mind is at rest. I leave no one to regret me much: I have only a father; and he is lately married, and will not miss me. By dying young, I shall escape great sufferings. I had not qualities or talents to make my way very well in the world: I should have been continually at fault.'

'But where are you going to, Helen? Can you see? Do you know?'

'I believe; I have faith: I am going to God.'

'Where is God? What is God?'

'My Maker and yours, who will never destroy what He created. I rely implicitly on His power, and confide wholly in His goodness: I count the hours till that eventful one arrives which shall restore me to Him, reveal Him to me.'

'You are sure, then, Helen, that there is such a place as heaven, and that our souls can get to it when we die?'

'I am sure there is a future state; I believe God is good; I can resign my immortal part to Him without any misgiving. God is my father; God is my friend: I love Him; I believe He loves me.'

'And shall I see you again, Helen, when I die?'

'You will come to the same region of happiness: be received by the same mighty, universal Parent, no doubt, dear Jane.'

Again I questioned, but this time only in thought. 'Where is that region? Does it exist?' And I clasped my arms closer round Helen; she seemed dearer to me than ever; I felt as if I could not let her go; I lay with my face hidden on her neck. Presently she said, in the sweetest tone –

'How comfortable I am! That last fit of coughing has tired me a little; I feel as if I could sleep: but don't leave me, Jane; I like to have you near me.'

'I'll stay with you, *dear* Helen: no one shall take me way.'

'Are you warm, darling?'

'Yes.'

'Good-night, Jane.'

'Good-night, Helen.'

She kissed me, and I her, and we both soon slumbered.

When I awoke it was day: an unusual movement roused me; I looked up; I was in somebody's arms; the nurse held me; she was carrying me through the passage back to the dormitory. I was not reprimanded for leaving my bed; people had something else to think about; no explanation was afforded then to my many questions; but a day or two afterwards I learned that Miss Temple, on returning to her own room at dawn, had found me laid in the little crib; my face against Helen Burns's shoulder, my arms round her neck. I was asleep, and Helen was – dead.

Her grave is in Brocklebridge churchyard: for fifteen years after her death it was only covered by a grassy mound; but now a grey marble tablet marks the spot, inscribed with her name, and the word '*Resurgam*'.

Questions

1   Describe the relationship between these two girls.

2   There is great sadness in this passage but also some hope of consolation for Jane. Do you agree with this statement? Explain with reference to the text.

3   Imagine you are Miss Temple. Write a diary extract based on the events outlined above.

D   Read the following passage from the novel *Circle of Friends* by Maeve Binchy and answer all four questions which follow.

Circle of Friends

Maeve Binchy

1949

The kitchen was full of the smells of baking. Benny put down her school bag and went on a tour of inspection.

'The cake hasn't been iced yet,' Patsy explained. 'The mistress will do that herself.'

'What are you going to put on it?' Benny was eager.

'I suppose Happy Birthday Benny.' Patsy was surprised.

'Maybe she'll put Benny Hogan, Ten.'

'I never saw that on a cake.'

'I think it is, when it's a big birthday like being ten.'

'Maybe.' Patsy said doubtful.

'And are the jellies made?'

'They're in the pantry. Don't go in poking them, you'll leave the mark of your finger and we'll all be killed.'

'I can't believe I'm going to be ten,' Benny said, delighted with herself.

'Ah, it's a big day all right.' Patsy spoke absently as she greased the trays for the queen cakes with a scrap of butter paper.

'What did you do when you were ten?'

'Don't you know with me every day was the same,' Patsy said cheerfully. 'There was no day different in the orphanage until I came out of it and came here.'

Benny loved to hear stories of the orphanage. She thought it was better than anything she read in books. There was the room with the twelve iron beds in it, the nice girls, the terrible girls, the time they all got nits in their hair and had to have their heads shaved.

'They must have had birthdays,' Benny insisted.

'I don't remember them,' Patsy sighed. 'There was a nice nun who said to me that I was Wednesday's child, full of woe.'

'That wasn't nice.'

'Well, at least she knew I was born on a Wednesday . . . Here's your mother, now let me get on with the work.'

Annabel Hogan came in carrying three big bags. She was surprised to see her daughter sitting swinging her legs in the kitchen.

'Aren't you home nice and early? Let me put these things upstairs.'

Benny ran over to Patsy when her mother's heavy tread was heard on the stairs.

'Do you think she got it?'

'Don't ask me, Benny, I know nothing.'

'You're saying that because you *do* know.'

'I *don't*. Really.'

'Was she in Dublin? Did she go up on the bus?'

'No, not at all.'

'But she must have.' Benny seemed very disappointed.

'No, she's not long gone at all . . . She was only up the town.'

Benny licked the spoon thoughtfully. 'It's nicer raw,' she said.

'You always thought that.' Patsy looked at her fondly.

'When I'm eighteen and can do what I like, I'll eat all my cakes uncooked,' Benny pronounced.

'No you won't, when you're eighteen you'll be so busy getting thin you won't eat cakes at all.'

'I'll always want cakes.'

'You say that now. Wait till you want some fellow to fancy you.'

'Do you want a fellow to fancy you?'

'Of course I do, what else is there?'

'What fellow? I don't want you to go, anyway.'

'I won't get a fellow, I'm from nowhere, a decent fellow wouldn't be able to talk about me and where I came from. I have no background, no life before, you see.'

'But you had a *great* life,' Benny cried. 'You'd make them all interested in you.'

There was no time to discuss it further. Benny's mother was back in the kitchen, her coat off and down to business with the icing sugar.

'Were you in Dublin at all today, Mother?'

'No, child, I had enough to do getting things ready for the party.'

'It's just I was wondering . . .'

'Parties don't run themselves, you know.' The words sounded sharp but the tone was kindly. Benny knew her mother was looking forward to it all too.

'And will Father be home for the cake bit?'

'Yes, he will. We've asked the people for half-past three, they'll all be here by four, so we needn't sit down to the tea until half-past five, and we wouldn't have got to the cake until you father has the business closed, and is back here.'

Benny's father ran Hogan's Outfitters, the big menswear shop in the middle of Knockglen. The shop was often at its busiest on a Saturday, when the farmers came in, or the men who had a half day themselves were marched in by wives to have themselves fitted out by Mr Hogan, or Mike the old assistant, the tailor who had been there since time immemorial. Since the days when young Mr Hogan had bought the business.

Questions

1   Compare and contrast the two characters of Benny and Patsy in this episode.

2   This story is set in Knockglen in Ireland in 1949. Which details help to establish the world of the story?

3   How would you describe the mood or atmosphere of this story? Explain your answer with close reference to the text.

4   This is the opening scene of a novel. Based on the passage above do you think you would like to read this book? Explain your answer.

E   Read carefully the following short story and then answer the questions which follow. The story is by Ray Bradbury and is called *August 2026:* 'There Will Come Soft Rains'.

August 2026: There Will Come Soft Rains
Ray Bradbury

In the living room the voice-clock sang, *Tick-tock, seven o'clock, time to get up, time to get up, seven o'clock!* as if it were afraid that nobody would. The morning house lay empty. The clock ticked on, repeating its sounds into the emptiness. *Seven-nine, breakfast time, seven-nine.*

In the kitchen the breakfast stove gave a hissing sigh and ejected from its warm interior eight pieces of perfectly browned toast, eight eggs sunny side up, sixteen slices of bacon, two coffees and two cool glasses of milk.

'Today is August 4, 2026,' said a second voice from the kitchen ceiling, 'in the city of Allendale, California.' It repeated the date three times for memory's sake. 'Today is Mr Featherstone's birthday. Today is the anniversary of Tilita's marriage. Insurance is payable, as are the water, gas, and light bills.'

Somewhere in the walls, relays clicked, memory tapes glided under electric eyes.

Eight-one, tick-tock, eight-one o'clock, off to school, off to work, run, run, eight-one! but no doors slammed, no carpets took the soft thread of rubber heels. It was raining outside.

The weather box on the front door sang quietly: 'Rain, rain, go away; rubbers, raincoats for today . . .' And the rain tapped on the empty house, echoing.

Outside, the garage chimed and lifted its door to reveal the waiting car. After a long wait the door swung down again.

At eight-thirty the eggs shrivelled and the toast was like stone. An aluminium wedge scraped them into the sink, where hot water whirled them down a metal throat which digested and flushed them away to the distant sea. The dirty dishes were dropped into a hot washer and emerged twinkling dry.

Nine-fifteen, sang the clock, *time to clean.*

Out of warrens in the wall, tiny robot mice darted. The rooms were a-crawl with the small cleaning animals, all rubber and metal. They thudded against chairs, whirling their moustached runners, kneading the rug nap, sucking gently at hidden dust. Then, like mysterious invaders, they popped into their burrows. Their pink electric eyes faded. The house was clean.

Ten o'clock. The sun came out from behind the rain. The house stood alone in a city of rubble and ashes. This was the one house left standing. At night the ruined city gave off a radioactive glow which could be seen for miles.

Ten-fifteen. The garden sprinklers whirled up in golden founts, filling the soft morning air with scatterings of brightness. The water pelted window-panes, running down the charred west side where the house had been burned evenly free of its white paint. The entire west face of the house was black, save for five places. Here the silhouette in paint of a man mowing a lawn. Here, as in a photograph, a woman bent to pick up flowers. Still farther over, their images burned on wood in one titanic instant, a small boy, hands flung into the air; higher up, the image of a thrown ball, and opposite him, a girl, hands raised to catch a ball which never came down.

The five spots of paint – the man, the woman, the children, the ball – remained. The rest was a thin charcoaled layer.

The gentle sprinkler rain filled the garden with falling light.

Until this day, how well the house had kept its peace. How carefully it had inquired, 'Who goes there? What's the password?' and, getting no answer from lonely foxes and whining cats, it had shut up its windows and drawn shades in an old-maidenly preoccupation with self-protection which bordered on mechanical paranoia.

It quivered at each sound, the house did. If a sparrow brushed a window the shade snapped up. The bird, startled, flew off! No, not even a bird must touch the house!

The house was an altar with ten thousand attendants, big, small, servicing, attending, in choirs. But the gods had gone away, and the ritual of the religion continued senselessly, uselessly.

Twelve noon.

A dog whined, shivering, on the front porch.

The front door recognized the dog voice and opened. The dog, once huge and fleshy, but now gone to bone and covered with sores, moved in and through the house, tracking mud. Behind it whirred angry mice, angry at having to pick up mud, angry at inconvenience.

For not a leaf fragment blew under the door but what the wall flipped open and the copper scrap rats flashed swiftly out. The offending dust, hair, or paper, seized in miniature steel jaws, was raced back to the burrows. There, down the tubes which fed into the cellar, it was dropped into the sighing vent of an incinerator which sat like evil Baal in a dark corner.

The dog ran upstairs, hysterically yelping to each door, at last realizing, as the house realized, that only silence was there.

It sniffed the air and scratched the kitchen door. Behind the door the stove was making pancakes which filled the house with a rich baked odour and the scent of maple syrup.

The dog frothed at the mouth, lying at the door, sniffing, its eyes turned to fire. It ran wildly in circles, biting at its tail, spun in a frenzy, and died. It lay in the parlour for an hour.

Two o'clock sang a voice.

Delicately sensing decay at last, the regiments of mice hummed out as softly as blown grey leaves in an electrical wind.

Two-fifteen.

The dog was gone.

In the cellar, the incinerator glowed suddenly and a whirl of sparks leaped up the chimney.

Two thirty-five.

Bridge tables sprouted from patio walls. Playing cards fluttered onto pads in a shower of pips. Martinis manifested on an oaken bench with egg-salad sandwiches. Music played.

But the tables were silent and the cards untouched.

At four o'clock the tables folded like butterflies back though the panelled walls.

Four-thirty.

The nursery walls glowed.

Animals took shape: yellow giraffes, blue lions, pink antelopes, lilac panthers cavorting in crystal substance. The walls were glass. They looked upon colour and fantasy. Hidden films clocked though well-oiled sprockets, and the walls lived. The nursery floor was woven to resemble a crisp, cereal meadow. Over this ran aluminium roaches and iron crickets, and in the hot, still air butterflies of delicate red tissue wavered among the sharp aroma of animal spoors! There was the sound like a great matted yellow hive of bees within a dark bellows, the lazy bumble of a purring lion. And there was the patter of okapi feet and the murmur of a fresh jungle rain, like other hoofs, falling upon the summer-starched grass. Now the walls dissolved into distances of parched weed, mile on mile, and the warm, endless sky. The animals drew away into thorn brakes and water holes.

It was the children's hour.

Five o'clock. The bath filled with clear hot water.

Six, seven, eight o'clock. The dinner dishes manipulated like magic tricks, and in the study a *click.* In the metal stand opposite the hearth where a fire now blazed up warmly, a cigar popped out, half an inch of soft grey ash on it, smoking, waiting.

Nine o'clock. The beds warmed their hidden circuits, for nights were cool here.

Nine five. A voice spoke from the study ceiling:

'Mrs McClellan, which poem would you like this evening?'

The house was silent.

The voice said at last, 'Since you express no preference, I shall select a poem at random.' Quiet music rose to back the voice. 'Sara Teasdale. As I recall, your favourite . . .'

There will come soft rains and the smell of the ground,
And swallows circling with their shimmering sound;

And frogs in the pools singing at night,
And wild plum trees in tremulous white;

Robins will wear their feathery fire,
Whistling their whims on a low fence-wire;

And not one will know of the war, not one
Will care at last when it is done,

Not one would mind, neither bird nor tree,
If mankind perished utterly;

And Spring herself, when she woke at dawn,
Would scarcely know that we were gone.

The fire burned on the stone hearth and the cigar fell away into a mound of quiet ash in its tray. The empty chairs faced each other between the silent walls, and the music played.

At ten o'clock the house began to die.

The wind blew. A falling tree bough crashed through the kitchen window. Cleaning solvent, bottled, shattered over the stove. The room was ablaze in an instant!

'Fire!' screamed a voice. The house-lights flashed, water pumps shot water from the ceilings. But the solvent spread on the linoleum, licking, eating, under the kitchen door, while the voices took it up in chorus: 'Fire, fire, fire!'

The house tried to save itself. Doors sprang tightly shut, but the windows were broken by the heat, and the wind blew and sucked upon the fire.

The house gave ground as the fire in ten billion angry sparks moved with flaming ease from room to room and then up the stairs. While scurrying water rats squeaked from the walls, pistolled their water, and ran for more. And the wall sprays let down showers of mechanical rain.

But too late. Somewhere, sighing, a pump shrugged to a stop. The quenching rain ceased. The reserve water supply which had filled baths and washed dishes for many quiet days was gone.

The fire crackled up the stairs. It fed upon Picassos and Matisses in the upper halls like delicacies, baking off the oily flesh, tenderly crisping the canvases into black shavings.

Questions
1   What features of this short story would make it suitable as the basis for a film? Explain the points you make through reference to the story.
2   'The central characters in this story are not human, yet we empathise with their plight.' Do you agree with this statement? Explain your answer.
3   What is ironic about Mrs McClellan's favourite poem?
4   Did you enjoy reading this story? Give reasons for your answer.

F   Read this excerpt from *Point Blanc* by Anthony Horovitz and answer the questions which follow.

Background to the extract

Alex Rider, a fourteen year old superspy, has been sent by MI6 to investigate Point Blanc school, a mysterious institute high in the Alps owned by Dr Grief. In the following passage Alex is fleeing the school on an improvised snowboard he made out of an ironing-board.

Point Blanc

Anthony Horovitz

Alex was on the edge of space, seemingly falling to certain death. In snowboarding language, he was catching air – meaning that he had shot away from the ground. Every ten metres he went forward, the mountainside disappeared another five metres downward. He felt the world spin around him. The wind whipped into his face. Then somehow he brought himself in line with the next section of the slope and shot down, steering the ironing-board ever further from Point Blanc. He was moving at a terrifying speed, trees and rock formations passing in a luminous green blur across his night-vision goggles. In some ways the steeper slopes made it easier. At one point he had tried to make a landing on a flat part of the mountain – a tabletop – to slow himself down. He had hit the ground with such a bone-shattering crash that he had nearly blacked out and had taken the next twenty metres almost totally blind.

The ironing-board was shuddering and shaking crazily and it took all his strength to make the turns. He was trying to follow the natural fall-line of the mountain but there were too many obstacles in the way. What he most dreaded was melted snow. If the board landed on a patch of mud at this speed, he would be thrown and killed. And he knew that the further down he went, the greater the danger would become.

But he had been travelling for five minutes and so far he had only fallen twice – both times into thick banks of snow that had protected him. How far down could it be? He tried to remember what James Sprintz had told him, but thinking was impossible at this speed. He was having to use every ounce of his conscious thought simply to stay upright.

He reached a small lip where the surface was level and drove the edge of the board into the snow, bringing himself to a skidding halt. Ahead of him the ground fell away alarmingly. He hardly dared look down. There were thick clumps of trees to the left and to the right. In the distance there was just a green blur. The goggles could only see so far.

And then he heard the noise coming up behind him. The scream of at least two – maybe more – engines. Alex looked back over his shoulder. For a moment there was nothing. But then he saw them – black flies swimming into his field of vision. There were two of them, heading his way.

Grief's men were riding specially adapted Yamaha Mountain Max snowmobiles equipped with 700cc triple-cylinder engines. The bikes were flying over the snow on their 141-inch tracks, effortlessly moving five times faster than Alex. The 300-watt headlights had already picked him out. Now the men sped towards him, cutting the distance between them with every second that passed.

Alex leapt forward, diving into the next slope. At the same moment, there was a sudden chatter, a series of distant cracks, and the snow leapt up all round him. Grief's men had machine-guns built into their snowmobiles! Alex yelled as he swooped down the mountainside, barely able to control the sheet of metal under his feet. The makeshift binding was tearing at his ankle. The whole thing was vibrating crazily. He couldn't see. He could only keep going, trying to keep his balance, hoping that the way ahead was clear.

The headlights of the nearest Yamaha shot out and Alex saw his own shadow stretch ahead of him on the snow. There was another chatter from the machine-gun and Alex ducked down, almost feeling the fan of bullets spray over his head. The second bike screamed up, coming parallel with him. He *had* to get off the mountainside. Otherwise he would be shot or run over. Or both.

He forced the board onto its edge, making a turn. He had seen a gap in the trees and he made for it. Now he was racing through the forest, with branches and trunks whipping past like crazy animations in a computer game. Could the snowmobiles follow him through here? The question was answered by another burst from the machine-guns, ripping through the leaves and branches. Alex searched for a narrower path. The board shuddered and he was almost thrown forward head first. The snow was getting thinner! He edged and turned, heading for two of the thickest trees. He passed between them with millimetres to spare. Now – follow that!

The Yamaha snowmobile had no choice. The rider had run out of paths. He was travelling too fast to stop. He tried to follow Alex between the trees, but the snowmobile was too wide. Alex heard a collision. There was a terrible crunch, then a scream, then an explosion. A ball of orange flame leapt over the trees, sending black shadows in a crazy dance. Ahead of him Alex saw another hillock and, beyond it, a gap in the trees. It was time to leave the forest.

He swooped up the hillock and out, once again catching air. As he left the trees behind him, two metres above the ground, he saw the second snowmobile. It had caught up with him. For a moment the two of them were side by side. Alex doubled forward and grabbed the nose of his board. Still in mid-air, he twisted the tip of the board, bringing the tail swinging round. He had timed it perfectly. The tail slammed into the second rider's head, almost throwing him out of his seat. The rider yelled and lost control. His snowmobile jerked sideways as if trying to make an impossibly tight turn. Then it left the ground, cartwheeling over and over again. The rider was thrown off, then screamed as the snowmobile completed its final turn and landed on top of him. Man and machine were bounced across the surface of the snow and then lay still. Alex slammed into the snow and skidded to a halt, his breath clouding green in front of his eyes.

1 What do you learn about Alex Rider from this passage?
2 Describe the conflict in this episode. How is this conflict resolved?
3 Anthony Horovitz is a popular children's writer. From your reading of this passage can you account for his popularity? Explain your answer.

STUDIED FICTION

The second part of the Fiction question will focus on the novel and short stories you have prepared in class with your teacher. Plot, character, narrator and the particular writing style of the author are the key areas to revise. Your answer should clearly identify the title of the novel or story and its author. Marks are awarded for accurate focus on the question asked, backed up with precise detail from the story. It is good but not essential to quote from the text, often a specific reference is sufficient for full marks.

Exam questions

Answer **either** 1 or 2 which follow.
1 Choose either the opening or the ending of a novel or short story you have studied.
  (a) Briefly describe what happens in the opening or the ending of your chosen text.
  (b) Did this opening or ending impress you? Explain your answer by reference to the novel or short story you have chosen. (30)

OR

2 From a novel or short story you have studied choose a character who experiences change.
  (a) Describe this character at the beginning of the novel or short story.
  (b) How has the character changed by the end of the novel or short story? Support your answer by reference to the text. (30)
  (2005, Paper 2, Section 3, Fiction)

Sample answers

Answer 1(a)

At the beginning of the novel *Of Mice and Men* by John Steinbeck we meet the hero George. He is described as being 'small and quick, dark of face, with restless eyes and sharp, strong features'. We realise that George is mentally the more alert of the two

Lennie and George from the film version of the novel *Of Mice and Men*.

characters as his friend Lennie is almost like a child in his innocence and simplicity. George assumes authority as he orders 'Lennie, for God's sakes don't drink so much'. This is how we learn that George is in charge and for the duration of the story this remains the case.

We also find out that although George has assumed responsibility for Lennie he is growing tired of the trouble they get into together. He tells him he could 'get along so easy and so nice' if he didn't have to take care of Lennie.

The most attractive side of his personality is his ability to weave a dreamlike spell over an audience by telling a story. Lennie begs him to 'Tell how it's gonna be'. George then describes a utopian farm, a fantasy home for the pair of them. He paints a very attractive picture of a house where the two men could 'build up a fire in the stove and set around it an' listen to the rain comin' down on the roof.' This is their dream, a place of their own where they will not be bothered by anyone, but instead enjoy simple comfort and security.

On the other hand, George is also realistic and in anticipation of further trouble tells Lennie to meet him at this spot if anything bad happens. This shows his ability to plan a strategy in order to avoid danger in the future.

Answer 1(b)
At the end of the novel George is still the wiser of the two men. He is still well able to tell a story as he uses the fantasy of their little farm with the rabbits to distract George while he shoots him. His plan to meet at this spot should any trouble arise proves to be helpful as George has accidentally killed Curley's wife and had to flee for his life.

The crucial difference in George is that he now realises there is no hope for Lennie. In the beginning he thought they could overcome the problems they had in Weed by running away to work in a different part of the country. Now he knows there is no point in running. This time Lennie has broken the law in a fatal way. By killing Curley's wife he has endangered his own life. He will be killed either by Curley and Carlson, or later by execution for the crime of murder. George appreciates how serious this is, but Lennie cannot fully understand his predicament. For this reason, George reluctantly decides to kill his good friend.

George has changed in another key way. He now has had to forsake his idyllic dream world. The farm where he and George and possibly old Candy would live in harmony feeding Lennie's rabbits and living off the 'fatta da lan" will never come to pass. George's dream is not going to happen and instead of a future of peace he must face the awful prospect of Lennie being cruelly killed for the crime of murder.

Previously when bad things happened George would give out to Lennie. At the end of the story when they meet in the woods beside the Salinas river Lennie asks him 'Ain't you gonna give me hell?' This time there is no need for George to scold Lennie. George has changed in his attitude towards his friend; it is pointless to try to teach him how to behave in the future.

Key points

In the studied fiction you must ensure that you have revised and learned certain key details of your novel and short story:

- The central characters, heroes and villains
- The setting for the story, time and place
- The main ideas explored by the writer, themes
- The key moments of the story, opening scenes, climax or confrontation and the resolution or ending of the story
- Your favourite scene, character
- Any lesson you learned from this story and how it might be applied to your own experience

If you have learned or highlighted significant quotations then you should try to include them as support in your answer. Otherwise full marks can still be attained by means of an answer which makes specific reference to key scenes from the story.

Remember: The most important point is to answer the question you are asked. For each point you make give a specific piece of evidence from the text and clarify what you mean by developing your idea into a short paragraph.

Coimisiún na Scrúduithe Stáit
State Examinations Commission

JUNIOR CERTIFICATE EXAMINATION, 2006

ENGLISH – HIGHER LEVEL – PAPER 1

180 marks

WEDNESDAY, 7 JUNE – MORNING, 9.30 – 12.00

**YOU MUST ATTEMPT ALL 4 SECTIONS
ON THIS PAPER**

**IT IS SUGGESTED THAT YOU SPEND ABOUT
HALF AN HOUR ON EACH OF SECTIONS
1, 3, 4, AND ABOUT ONE HOUR ON
SECTION 2**

READING

Read carefully the following passage by Anthony Glavin and then answer the questions that follow.

This passage is an edited version of what was originally broadcast on the RTÉ Radio One programme, 'Sunday Miscellany'.

In Praise of Goldfish

There is a lot to be said for goldfish as childhood pets – especially when the care and feeding of a pet reverts to parents, as so often happens. Compared to a dog, which needs walking, or a cat, which needs to be let out-and-in-and-out-again, a goldfish is very much a low maintenance affair.

I know of what I speak as our goldfish, Guinny – short for Guinevere, has been in my charge for several years now. To be fair, our daughters looked after Guinny and her consort Lancelot when the couple first came to us, inherited from a younger cousin who had lost all interest in them at home. But now every time she visits us she asks eagerly, 'Can I feed the fish?' And it was our elder daughter who named them Guinevere and Lancelot, inspired by the Arthurian legends she was reading that summer.

Lancelot passed away a year after he came to us, but Guinny's still going strong, somewhere into her fifth year, we reckon. Though whether it's actually *her* and not *his* fifth year isn't absolutely clear, as Guinevere and Lancelot were named according to size with Lancelot, being the larger. Although now solo in her bowl, Guinny is not our only family pet; she shares that pleasure with our playful cat, Esmerelda. Traditionally, cats and fish have been portrayed as enemies. However, unlike the animosity between cats and mice, the entertainment potential of cats versus goldfish has never been exploited. It is easy to see why. What hope would there be for a cartoon series where a cat relentlessly pursued a goldfish with the aim of eating it? In its own element of water the goldfish could disdainfully take refuge in an underwater castle or under a fake treasure chest. But who would find that entertaining? What chance for a thrilling chase around the cramped interior of even the most spacious fish tank? The alternative, with the conflict taking place in the cat's element of air, is worse still, with the goldfish hopelessly outclassed and capable only of flopping about helplessly making wheezing noises. Tom and Jerry have nothing to fear from Tom and Goldie!

Goldfish have evolved a long way from the freshwater carp first domesticated by the Chinese over a thousand years ago. The novelty of golden fish was first reserved for the aristocracy but by the fourteenth century few Chinese households were so poor that they could not afford a few goldfish. The transfer of the species from Asia to Europe by slow sailing ships is testimony to the endurance and adaptability of these animals. The exact date of this dispersal is uncertain, but it was early in the eighteenth century. By mid-century there were many European goldfish devotees, and, over time, breeders have developed countless varieties: ones with bulging eyes, double and triple fins, strange tails, and vivid colours – although most so-called goldfish are actually orange. These graceful creatures are now among the most popular pets in the world, though the exotic colours of today's varieties makes it is hard to imagine their origins in the dull-brown domestic carp.

It is said that the goldfish has a memory span of three seconds, though I sometimes wonder how ichthyologists – scientists who study fish – measure for memory. Or, for that matter, for IQ, given that goldfish are also said to be highly intelligent and able to recognise who in a household feeds them, greeting their friend upon sight by swimming briskly about the bowl. Certainly that's true for our Guinny, who lashes about whenever she sees me pass by. What's more, we have developed a neat routine in which she (or is it he?) rises to the top of the bowl to accept the massive pellet of fish food I've rolled between my fingers.

It seems goldfish can live for up to fifteen years, sometimes developing such a bond with humans that their piscine passing can be quite traumatic for all concerned. A neighbour recently told me of the morning his pair expired and swam off to that great fishbowl in the sky. He related how his wife immediately sent him into town for an identical pair before their son awoke, only for the four-year-old to meet his father coming in the gate, a plastic water-filled bag in his hand. 'What are you doing with those fish, Dad?' the little lad shouted all amazed.

'Oh, just taking them for a walk, son,' my neighbour calmly replied!

Answer the following **four** questions:

1.   Why does the writer recommend a goldfish as a pet? Support your answer with evidence from the **first** paragraph of the passage.   (10)

2.   What historical facts about goldfish do you learn from reading this passage?   (10)

3.   The author is dismissive of the idea of a cartoon based on the traditional animosity between cats and fish. Do you agree with him? Give reasons for your answer, based on the **third** paragraph of the passage.   (10)

4.   Did you find this passage entertaining? Give reasons for your answer.   (10)

SECTION 2:   PERSONAL WRITING   [70]

Write a prose composition on any **one** of the following titles. Except where otherwise stated, you are free to write in any form you wish e.g. narrative, descriptive, dramatic, short story, etc.

1. The pet (real or imaginary) that I would most like to keep.

2. The talking goldfish.

3. Fictional characters I would like to meet.

4. A day in my life that I would like to relive.

5. Write a composition including the line, 'It had been a lot of hard work and had taken ages but, in the end, it was worth the effort.'

6. Everyone deserves a second chance.

7. Look at the picture below and write a composition inspired by it.

8. Write a speech for or against the motion: 'Having a job during the school year is bad for Second Level students.'

SECTION 3: FUNCTIONAL WRITING [30]

Answer **either** Question 1 **or** Question 2.

You will be rewarded for:

- Well-structured answers
- Clarity of expression
- An appropriate tone
- Good grammar, spelling and punctuation.

1. A national newspaper has organised a 'Person of the Year' award. Write a letter to the editor nominating the person you think is most deserving of this award. You should explain why you think this person deserves the award.

OR

2. Most books and DVDs have a short blurb on the outside of the back cover. Typically this is a brief text which describes and praises the plot, characterisation, acting, etc. Write such a blurb for any book or DVD of your choice.

SECTION 4: MEDIA STUDIES [40]

Examine carefully the advertisement that appears below.

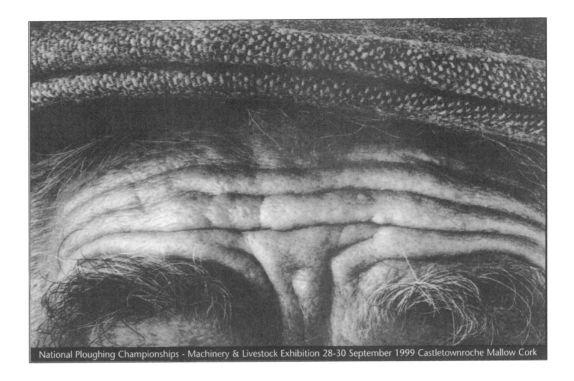

National Ploughing Championships - Machinery & Livestock Exhibition 28-30 September 1999 Castletownroche Mallow Cork

1. (a) This advertisement – for the 1999 National Ploughing Championships –
        provides the reader with very little written text. Much of what the advertisers
        want to communicate is conveyed visually. What do you think is
        communicated about the event by the picture?   (20)

    (b) Do you think this advertisement is effective in promoting the event? Explain
        your answer with reference to the advertisement.   (20)

Coimisiún na Scrúduithe Stáit
State Examinations Commission

JUNIOR CERTIFICATE EXAMINATION, 2006

ENGLISH – HIGHER LEVEL – PAPER 2
180 marks

WEDNESDAY, 7 JUNE – AFTERNOON, 1.30 – 4.00

YOU MUST ATTEMPT ALL THREE SECTIONS ON THIS PAPER

EACH SECTION CARRIES 60 MARKS.

SPEND ABOUT 45 MINUTES ON EACH SECTION

SECTION 1:   DRAMA   [60]

Answer QUESTION ONE and QUESTION TWO

QUESTION ONE   (30)

Answer either (A) or (B).

(A) SHAKESPEAREAN DRAMA

The following extract (in edited form) is taken from *The Winter's Tale* by William Shakespeare. Read the extract carefully and then answer the questions which follow.

> **Background to the extract:**
> Leontes, the King of Sicily, believes that Perdita, a newly born royal baby, is not his daughter. He sends Antigonus, one of his noblemen, on a dangerous sea voyage to Bohemia with instructions to leave the baby there with a box containing papers and jewels. As Antigonus approaches Bohemia, a violent storm drives his ship onto the rocks. He escapes ashore with the baby and the box, and hears a group of young noblemen hunting bears nearby. Being fearful of both the storm and the bear-hunt Antigonus abandons the baby and the box.

Scene: The Seashore

Old Shepherd: (*hearing bear hunt*)I wish there were no age between ten and three-and-twenty, for there is nothing between those years but wronging the old, stealing, fighting and chasing women. Hark you now, nobody but these boiled-brains of nineteen and two-and-twenty would hunt in this weather! They have scared away two of my best sheep, which I fear the wolf will sooner find than the master.

Suddenly he stops as he sees the baby.

What have we here? Mercy on us all – a baby!
A very pretty baby. A boy or a girl, I wonder?
A pretty one, a very pretty girl. I'll take her up for pity. Or maybe yet I'll wait until my son comes.
I heard him nearby just now.

Enter Son in a state of terror, having seen Antigonus's ship tossed in the storm, and the fleeing Antigonus attacked by a bear.

Son:	Oh my God!
Old Shepherd:	(*alarmed*) Come hither. What ail'st thou, man?
Son:	(*dolefully*) I have seen two such sights by sea and by land!

Because of the terrible storm I cannot say it is a sea, for it is now married with the sky.

Old Shepherd:	Why, boy, how is it?
Son:	I would you did but see how it storms, how it rages, how it takes up the shore.

Oh, the most piteous cry of the poor souls trapped aboard that ship! Sometimes to see 'em and not to see 'em;

Now the ship clawing the moon with her mainmast, then swallowed with froth.

And then on the land, to see how the bear tore out the man's shoulder-bone, how he cried to me for help, and said his name was Antigonus.

But to finish off the ship – to see how the sea flap-dragoned it!
But first how the poor souls roared, and the sea mocked them, and how the poor gentleman roared and the bear mocked him, both roaring louder than the wind.

Old Shepherd:	Name of mercy, when was this, boy?
Son:	Now, now. I have not winked since I saw these sights.

The men are not yet cold under water, nor the bear half-dined on the gentleman.

He's at him now.

Old Shepherd:	Would I have been by to have helped the man!

Heavy matters, heavy matters . . .

But look thee here, boy. Now bless thyself.
You met with the dying, and I with the living. Here's a sight for thee. Look thee.

Shows the baby to his son

And look thee here. (*pointing to the box beside the baby*)

	Take up the box, boy, take up the box. Open it.
	The fairies told me I'd be rich. Open it. What's within, boy?
Son:	(*opening the box*) Oh father, look thee, papers and riches beyond thought!
	The sins of your youth are forgiven!
Old Shepherd:	Home. . . home the quickest way! We must hide this box.
	We are lucky, boy! We need no longer tend the sheep.
Son:	You go home. I'll go and see if the bear is done with the gentleman, and how much of him he hath eaten. If there be any of him left, I'll bury him.
Old Shepherd:	That's a good deed. 'Tis a lucky day, boy, and we'll do good deeds on't.

Answer **two** of the following questions. Each question is worth 15 marks.

1. What impression do you get of the old shepherd *or* the son from this extract? Support your answer with reference to the text.

2. Basing your answer on evidence from the above extract how do you think the old shepherd's life and that of his son will be changed as a result of discovering Perdita and the box.

3. If this extract is to be staged and you are in charge of sound effects **OR** lighting, write an account of *how* and *why* you would use particular sound effects **OR** particular lighting effects in this drama. Support your answer with reference to the text.

(B) OTHER DRAMA

The following extract (in edited form) is taken from a version of the play *Everyman* by Obudtunde Ljimere.

> **Background to the extract:**
> Everyman, Companion and Poor Neighbour, three of the characters in the play, are standing in front of Everyman's house. Everyman is talking with his friend, Companion, when Poor Neighbour approaches fearfully.

Everyman:	(*speaking to Companion*) You, my friend and companion of many years, take this money and hurry down to Bisi, my lady friend.
	Tell her to come to my party and bring the best musical band she can find. And give her these few notes, for these independent women and lip-painted ladies have many needs and great pride.
	Let her go and buy what she desires and let her heart be happy when she comes. This money will get her velvet cloth, sarasobia scent, rekyirekyi, gold and silver, head-ties, handkerchiefs, umbrella, shoes, shirt and blouse, iron bed, blanket and bed sheets, pillows and pillow-cases, sleeping-gowns, easy chairs, door blinds, window blinds, mosquito-net, table and table-cloth, carpets, bed curtains, hand-watch, looking-glass, powder, sewing-machine, travelling cases, bicycle, record player and so many other things a woman could use.
Poor Neighbour:	(*bowing low before Everyman*) Master, I beg you, help me. I am in trouble.
Companion:	Do you know this man?
Everyman:	Who are you? I don't remember seeing you before.
Poor Neighbour:	I am Adeleke, Sir, the son of Kunle. I have known better days than these, Sir. I was your neighbour once.
	Lived in that pretty house right next door.
	But I ran into debt and was driven out!
Everyman:	All right, all right! *(he hands him a coin)*
Poor Neighbour:	(*refusing the coin*) Three pence? That is a poor gift. If you would

	share that wad of notes with me, my worries could be over.
Companion:	If you give him more, you will have a thousand beggars after you tomorrow!
Poor Neighbour:	This money, I know, is nothing to you. If you spend it ten times over, you only need to beckon your servant and he will bring you the same amount from your house.
Everyman:	You foolish man! Do you know what it means to be a rich man? Do you think it is easy?

'A rich man!' That is easily said. But we rich people lead a hard life.
If you knew it you might not want to change with me.
My money can never sit still.
It must run here and there, work for me and travel and fight.
Money must marry more money and get pregnant with more money.
A rich man has no easy life: his lorries break down and want to be mended.
The price of cocoa falls and petrol goes up.
One's children go to school, they study abroad, gifts of money must be given when they marry.
Do you think it is easy to maintain all these houses and cars and farms, families and servants?
Do you think that money grows on trees? No work is harder than collecting debts and rents!

Suppose my property was divided equally
among all those who are in need,
do you think your share
would be bigger than these three pence here?

Everyman throws down the three pence. Poor Neighbour picks them up and leaves.

| Companion: | You answered him well, you put him in his place! Money makes a man wise. |
| | I can see that indeed. |

Answer **two** of the following questions. Each question is worth 15 marks.

1.   What do you learn about the character of Everyman from this scene? Support your answer with reference to the text.

2.   Imagine you are Bisi *or* Companion *or* Poor Neighbour. Briefly describe the type of life you lead, based on evidence from the above extract.

3.   This extract is to be staged and you are the Director. How would you direct this scene with reference to **one** of the following:
      (a)   Gestures by the actors
      (b)   Costume/Dress to be worn by the actors
      (c)   How the characters should speak their lines.

QUESTION TWO   (30)

Answer **EITHER 1 OR 2.**

N.B. You must give the name of the play that you choose. You may **NOT** choose either of the scenes quoted on this examination paper as the basis for your answer.

1.   Consider a character from a play you have studied. Choose a significant time of *either* good luck *or* bad luck which this character experiences.
      (a)   Briefly describe this experience of good luck *or* bad luck.
      (b)   Discuss how the character deals with it in the play.

OR

2.   'Plays teach us lessons about life.'
      Choose any play you have studied and explain how it has made you aware of any one of the following:

Love *or* Death *or* Conflict *or* Harmony.

      Explain your answer by reference to your chosen play.

SECTION 2:   POETRY   [30]

Read the following poem (in edited form) by Mark Roper and answer the questions which follow.

Van Gogh's Yellow Chair

Mark Roper

I would love to sit
in the yellow chair
in the painting

when a shadow lies
like a shy animal
in a corner

and the day's air
is like water in which
small noises swim.

I would sit there
safe from harm
safe from all surprise.

Beyond the frame
on every side
the outside world

would open wide
but I'd have crossed
the great divide

so long as I never
rose from
that yellow chair.

Answer QUESTION ONE and QUESTION TWO

QUESTION ONE   (30)

Answer any TWO of the following questions. Each question is worth 15 marks.

1. 'I would love to sit
   in the yellow chair
   in the painting . . .'
   What is so appealing about Van Gogh's yellow chair, according to the speaker? Explain your answer with reference to the poem.

2. In your own words explain what is being said in the last three stanzas.

3. What is your favourite image from the poem? Explain your choice.

QUESTION TWO   (30)

Answer **EITHER 1 OR 2**.
N.B. In answering you may **NOT** use the poem given on this paper. You must give the title of the poem you choose and the name of the poet.

1. Take any poem you have studied which deals with wishes *or* thoughts.
   (a) What are the poet's main wishes **OR** thoughts in the poem?
   (b) Describe how *either* the imagery *or* the language of the poem contributes to the poet's expression of his/her thoughts or wishes. Explain your answer with reference to the poem.   (30)

OR

2. If you could invite a poet of your choice to your school, who would you choose?
   (a) Explain your choice of poet with reference to the poet's work.
   (b) Choose your favourite poem by this poet and explain why you like it so much. Support your answer by reference to the poem.   (30)

SECTION 3:   FICTION   [60]

Read the following extract (in edited form) from the novel *Stone Cold* by Robert Swindells and then answer the questions that follow.

You can call me Link. It's not my name, but it is what I say when anybody asks, which isn't often. I'm invisible, see? One of the invisible people. Right now I'm sitting in a doorway watching the passers-by. They avoid looking at me. They're afraid I want something they've got, and they're right. Also, they don't want to think about me. They don't like reminding themselves that I exist. Me, and those like me. We're living proof that everything's not all right and we make the place untidy. Hang about and I'll tell you the story of my fascinating life . . .

We sat in St. James's till two o'clock. It wasn't warm, but we were out of the wind. Then Ginger said, 'I'm gonna try round the square for a while. . . coming?' I nodded. 'If it's okay with you. It's time I had a go at getting some cash by myself, but I'll feel better if you are somewhere around.' He nodded. 'Fair enough. Tell you what – you try outside the National Gallery. It's not exactly the height of the tourist season but there are always people about, and you can see into the square from the steps.'

The Gallery wasn't fantastically busy but there was a steady trickle of people going in and out. Some were sitting on the steps in spite of the cold. Ginger left me there. I watched him merge with the crowd, and then turned my attention to the business of the day.

It was hard at first. Really hard. I stood, watching people pass, trying to spot a likely punter. God knows what I was looking for – a kind face, I suppose, or at least someone who didn't look as though he'd swear at me or punch me in the mouth. It was futile, of course. You can't read people's characters in their faces. You never know what a punter's reaction is going to be; but I didn't know that then. Finally, I steeled myself and asked a guy at random. He growled, 'Not a chance,' and bounded up the steps, taking them two at a time. I wasted the next five minutes feeling hurt. Rejected. I asked myself how it was possible for a person to be sensitive to the beauty of fine art, and at the same time insensitive to the feelings of a fellow creature. I took it personally, which is fatal. After a while I realised this and began choosing guys and women at random, expecting nothing, telling them to have a nice day whether they gave or refused. I blunted the point of my own sensitivity in the flinty soil of their indifference until I too became indifferent, and after that it was easier.

I worked till the Gallery closed, sometimes standing and sometimes sitting on the steps. My feet became numb and I was half frozen but I stuck at it, and when the place closed at dusk and the punters drifted away I counted up and found I'd collected just under four Euro. I stumped across to the Square and found Ginger slumped on a bench. He looked up as I approached, 'I'm frozen to the bone', he said, 'let's eat'. We got pizza slices and coke.

We ended up in the doorway of a shop, huddled in our bags.

If you think sleeping rough's just a matter of finding a dry spot where the police won't move you on and getting your head down, you're wrong. Not your fault, of course – if you've never tried it you've no way of knowing what it's like, so maybe I'll talk you through a typical night.

You pick your spot. Usually it's going to have a floor of stone, tile, concrete or brick. In other words it's going to be hard and cold. It might be a bit cramped, too – shop doorways often are. And remember, if it's winter you're going to be half frozen before you even start. Anyway, you've got your place, and if you're lucky enough to have a sleeping-bag you unroll it and get in.

Settled for the night? Well maybe, maybe not.

Answer **QUESTION ONE** and **QUESTION TWO**

QUESTION ONE   (30)

Answer two of the following questions. Each question is worth 15 marks.

1. Link says he is one of the 'invisible people'. Do you agree with him? Explain your answer by reference to the extract.

2. Does the character of Link appeal to you? Explain your reasons with reference to the text.

3. 'Settled for the night? Well maybe, maybe not.' Basing your views on what you have found in the text, why do you think Link might have said this?

QUESTION TWO   (30)

Answer **EITHER 1 OR 2.**

N.B. In answering you may **NOT** use the extract given above as the basis for your answer. You must give the title of the text you choose and the name of the author.

1.   Choose a novel **OR** short story that has a strong sense of place *or* setting.
     (a)   Describe this place *or* setting.   (15)
     (b)   How is this place *or* setting important in the novel or short story you have
           chosen?
     Support your answer with reference to the novel or short story.   (15)

OR

2.   From a novel **OR** short story you have studied, choose a character you would *either*
     like to be *or* not like to be.
     Explain your choice of character with reference to your chosen text. (30)

Coimisiún na Scrúduithe Stáit
State Examinations Commission

JUNIOR CERTIFICATE EXAMINATION, 2007

ENGLISH – HIGHER LEVEL – PAPER 1

180 marks

WEDNESDAY, 6 JUNE – MORNING, 9.30 – 12.00

**YOU MUST ATTEMPT ALL 4 SECTIONS
ON THIS PAPER**

**IT IS SUGGESTED THAT YOU SPEND ABOUT
HALF AN HOUR ON EACH OF SECTIONS
1, 3, 4, AND ABOUT ONE HOUR ON
SECTION 2**

SECTION 1: READING [40]

Read carefully the following article (in edited form) by Christopher Frayling and then answer the questions that follow.

Capturing the Image of Science on Film

1. Most of the scientists portrayed on the big screen have been mad, bad or dangerous to know. The roll-call includes doctors Frankenstein, Jekyll and Strangelove, and goes right back to the origins of cinema as fairground entertainment.

2. The pioneer French animator Georges Meiles featured numerous top-hatted, umbrella-waving astronomers and engineers in his early shorts, and they all came over as vaudeville turns. The first ever version of Frankenstein was made in 1910, for Edison's studio; the "creature" of the novel turned into a pantomime "monster", who emerged from an alchemist's cauldron.

    There were a few ever-so-noble 1930s and 1940s biopics such as *Louis Pasteur* and *Madame Curie*. These were the sort of films that attracted Academy Awards, and gave work to characters who liked dressing up in lab-coats and mutton-chop whiskers and looking through microscopes. But, mostly, films have told audiences that science and technology are likely to be very bad for them.

    Do these images matter? How do they relate to the agenda of anxiety presented daily by the media? Why is it that though the particular science may change – poison gas in the 1920s, medicine in the 1930s, nuclear physics in the 1950s, biology since the 1980s – the stereotype has remained so constant?

3. Forty years ago, David Wade Chambers conducted a celebrated project in which he asked 4807 schoolchildren aged 5–11 in the Montreal area to draw a scientist without hesitating. Their gut reaction was, especially among the 9–11 year olds, to resort to the off-the-shelf cultural stereotype: Einstein hair, coke bottle spectacles, white lab-coat, bubbling glassware and in some cases a door marked "secret". The scientists were also male (only 28 out of 2000 girls surveyed drew a female). A couple of years ago I arranged a similar smaller scale test at a school in England. I honestly thought the findings would have changed. After all, in recent years heroic scientists – albeit mavericks who take on the establishment – have become more common in film, not to mention the gungho attitude towards technological progress in *Star Trek*, *Star Wars* and countless comic-book derivatives.

4. I was wrong. Roughly the same proportion of 9–11 year olds drew lunatic or manic

scientists in white lab-coats – although there were more female lunatics, the scientists were younger and they wore branded t-shirts or shoes. The style of drawing owed more to cheap sci-fi animation and a new character had appeared: the laboratory rat. Also, the stereotyping seemed to be starting younger – among the 7–9 year olds. Here was a clue perhaps. The 1960s movie stereotype had migrated towards children's cartoons, comics, computer games and stand-up comedians (Eddie Murphy as *The Nutty Professor*, Steve Martin as *The Man With Two Brains*).

5. I've tried to track the origins of the stereotype's main components: the hair, the disability, the lab-coat and the glassware, because these are evidently cultural phenomena. The person who actually taught the children science was a woman, she didn't wear a lab-coat or spectacles, bubbling glassware was discouraged and there were no laboratory rats. So the stereotype is being carried by the culture rather than by personal experience.

6. The frizzy hair of course comes via Albert Einstein – a symbol of the brilliant but unruly brain beneath it. Einstein still has the highest recognition factor worldwide of any scientist of the modern era. His playful and awe-inspiring image has come to stand for the good eccentric scientist who may be incomprehensible but is somehow doing good for us all. Einstein's kindly and wise eyes were copied for the design of ET's; his forehead was the inspiration for Yoda's in *Star Wars*. Even his hair has survived on such admirable, eccentric film characters as the original Doctor Who, Doc Brown in *Back to the Future* (1985), and Einstein in the 1995 movie *IQ*.

Answer the following **three** questions:

1. "Mostly films have told audiences that science and technology are likely to be very bad for them."

    What evidence can you find in paragraph 1 and 2 of the passage in support of this statement? (10)

2. Research has discovered that there has been very little change over the years in the style of drawing used by children to represent scientists.

    (a) What changes are outlined in paragraph 4 of the passage? (5)

    (b) What, according to the author, has influenced the children's style of drawing scientists? (10)

3. (a) Outline the stereotypical image of scientists given in paragraph 5. (5)

    (b) Do you think that this image is a fair or accurate one? (10)

SECTION 2:   PERSONAL WRITING   [70]

Write a prose composition on any **one** of the following titles. Except where otherwise stated, you are free to write in any form you wish e.g. narrative, descriptive, dramatic, short story, etc.

1.   A teenager's guide to life.

2.   You are an alien visiting earth for a day. Write about your experiences, especially your reaction to human behaviour.

3.   How best to spend a Saturday afternoon.

4.   Science's contribution to the modern world – a mixed blessing.

5.   Write a speech for **OR** against the motion, "Second level education in Ireland is a good preparation for life".

6.   "The day started the same as any other, nobody could have known that by evening …"

      Continue this story.

7.   As a result of an accident in chemistry class your teacher has shrunk to a fraction of his/her normal size.
      WHAT HAPPENED NEXT

SECTION 3:   FUNCTIONAL WRITING   [30]

1.   Look at the material on the next page adapted from the Irish Cancer Society's Sun Smart campaign. Write a set of instructions – one instruction for each picture – designed to help people enjoy the summer sun safely.
      (Make sure to put the number of each picture beside the instruction associated with it.)

How to be Sun Smart

The sun produces ultraviolet radiation that is harmful to human skin and can lead to skin cancer. The good news is that taking a few simple measures can prevent much of this damage. Common sense would suggest protecting the skin from the sun, especially during those times of the day when the sun is hottest.

Picture 1   Picture 2   Picture 3

Picture 4   Picture 5   Picture 6

OR

2.   Write a list of safety guidelines to be displayed on a poster **EITHER** in your school's Science Lab **OR** in the Woodwork, Metalwork or Home Economics room.

SECTION 4:   MEDIA STUDIES   [40]

Martyn Turner's cartoon below shows aliens viewing planet Earth in the future. Examine the cartoon and

(a) State briefly what you think the cartoonist's message is.   (20)

(b) Imagine that one of the aliens in the cartoon is a journalist. Write a brief article that he/she/it might write for the front page of *The Martian Times* on his/her/its return home.   (20)

Note: The Stern Report mentioned in the cartoon refers to a recent report by economist Sir Nicholas Stern on the effect of human activity, such as global warming, on the world's climate.

OR

1.   (a) Write the text for a radio advertisement for a new chocolate bar called "Yummy". Remember the message is going to be heard not seen.   (20)

     (b) Suggest the type of voice most appropriate for the voice-over for your advertisement. Indicate any music or sound effects you think might make it more effective. Explain your choices.   (20)

Coimisiún na Scrúduithe Stáit
State Examinations Commission

JUNIOR CERTIFICATE EXAMINATION, 2007

ENGLISH – HIGHER LEVEL – PAPER 2

180 marks

WEDNESDAY, 6 JUNE – AFTERNOON 1.30–4.00

YOU MUST ATTEMPT ALL THREE SECTIONS ON
THIS PAPER

EACH SECTION CARRIES 60 MARKS.

SPEND ABOUT 45 MINUTES ON EACH SECTION

SECTION 1:　　　　　　DRAMA　　　　　　　[60]

Answer QUESTION ONE and QUESTION TWO

QUESTION ONE　　　　　　　　　(30)

Answer either **(A) or (B)**.

(A)　SHAKESPEAREAN DRAMA

The following extract (in edited form) is taken from *The Taming of the Shrew* by William Shakespeare. Read the extract carefully and then answer the questions which follow.

> **Background to this extract:**
> Katharina is the wild, rough and troublesome elder daughter of Baptista. Baptista wants to find a husband for her. He has arranged a marriage with Petruchio, a nobleman. In this extract Katharina and Petruchio have just met for the first time.

Note: In Shakespeare's time a woman with a scolding or nagging nature was called a **shrew**.

Petruchio:	[*He seizes her in his arms*] Nay, come, Kate, come; you must not look so sour.
Katharina:	[*She struggles*] It is my fashion when I see a crab.*
Petruchio:	Why, here's no crab, and therefore look not sour.
Katharina:	There is, there is.
Petruchio:	Then show it me.
Katharina:	Had I a glass I would.
Petruchio:	What, you mean my face? By Saint George, I am too young for you.
Katharina:	Yet you are withered.
Petruchio:	[*Kisses her hand*] 'Tis with cares.
Katharina:	[*She slips from him*] I care not!
Petruchio:	Nay, hear you Kate. In sooth, you escape not so. [*He catches her once more*]
Katharina:	I'll scrape you if I tarry. Let me go! [*She struggles again, biting and scratching as he speaks*]
Petruchio:	No, not a whit – I find you passing gentle: 'Twas told me you were rough and coy and sullen, And now I find reports of you untrue; For thou art pleasant, lively, passing courteous,

	But slow in speech; yet sweet as spring-time flowers.
	Thou canst not frown, thou canst not look unkindly,
	Nor bite the lip, as angry wenches will,
	Nor hast thou pleasure to be cross in talk;
	But thou with mildness entertain'st thy admirers,
	With gentle ways, soft and agreeable. [*He releases her*]
	Kate like the hazel-twig
	Is straight and slender, and as brown in hue
	As hazel-nuts and sweeter than the kernels …
Katharina:	Go, fool! Order your servants about, not me.
Petruchio:	Did ever the Goddess Diana so grace a place
	As Kate this chamber with her noble ways?
	O, be thou Diana and let her be Kate.
Katharina:	Where did you study all this goodly speech?
Petruchio:	It comes naturally, from my mother-wit.
Katharina:	A witty mother! And without wit her son!
Petruchio:	Setting all this chat aside, your father hath consented
	That you shall be my wife; your dowry agreed on;
	And you, willing or not, will marry me.
	Now, Kate, I am a husband fit for you
	For by this light whereby I see thy beauty,
	– Thy beauty that doth make me like thee well -
	Thou must be married to no man but me.
	For I am born to tame you, Kate,
	And bring you from a wild Kate to a Kate
	As kind as other household Kates.

* Crab: Crap-apple, sour fruit

Answer **two** of the following questions. Each question is worth 15 marks.

1. What is your impression of Katharina from this extract? Support your answer with reference to the text.

2. Do you think Petruchio's way of speaking to Katharina would encourage her to marry him? Base your answer on this extract.

3. Imagine that you are directing this play. In the context of the extract you have read above give your thoughts on **two** of the following aspects of your production: use of voice, costuming, setting, movement on stage.

(B) OTHER DRAMA

The following extract (in edited form) is from the play *Galileo* by Bertolt Brecht. Read the extract carefully and answer the questions which follow.

> **Background to this extract:**
> Children are playing in the street. The children are convinced that one of the occupants of the house in the street is a witch. They mistake the shadow of a soup ladle she is using for a broomstick. At this moment they meet Andrea, a university scholar.

The window of a small house is still lit, and a big grotesque shadow, like an old witch and her cauldron, falls upon the house wall beyond. Barefoot CHILDREN *in rags see the shadow and point to the little house.*

CHILDREN (*singing*):
    One, two, three, four, five, six,
    Old Martina is a witch.
    At night, on a broomstick she sits
    And on the church steeple she spits.

One of the BOYS, *pushed forward by the others, creeps up to the little house from which the shadow comes, and steals the occupant's milk which has been left on the doorstep.*

ANDREA (*quietly*): What are you doing with that milk?
BOY (*stopping in mid-movement*): She is a witch.

The other CHILDREN *run away.*

ANDREA: Hmm! And because she is a witch she mustn't have milk? Is that the idea?
BOY: Yes.
ANDREA: And how do you know she is a witch?
BOY (*points to shadow on house wall*): Look!
ANDREA: Oh! I see.
BOY: And she rides on a broomstick at night – and she bewitches the coachman's horses. My cousin Luigi looked through the hole in the stable roof, that the snow storm made, and heard the horses coughing something terrible.

ANDREA: Oh! How big was the hole in the stable roof?

BOY: Luigi didn't tell. Why?

ANDREA: I was asking because maybe the horses got sick because it was cold in the stable. You had better ask Luigi how big that hole is.

BOY: You are not going to say Old Martina isn't a witch because you can't.

ANDREA: No. I can't say she isn't a witch. I haven't looked into it. A man can't know about a thing he hasn't looked into, or can he?

BOY: No! But THAT! (*He points to the shadow.*) She is stirring Hellbroth.

ANDREA: Lets see. Do you want to have a look? I can lift you up.

BOY: You can lift me to the window, mister! (*He takes a sling-shot out of his pocket*) I can really bash her from there.

ANDREA: Hadn't we better make sure she is a witch before we shoot? (*Taking the sling-shot from the boy*) I'll hold that.

The BOY *puts the milk jug down and follows* ANDREA *reluctantly to the window.* ANDREA *lifts the boy up so that he can look in.*

ANDREA: What do you see?

BOY (*slowly*): Just an old girl cooking porridge.

ANDREA: Oh! Nothing to it then. Now look at her shadow.

The BOY *looks over his shoulder and back and compares the reality and the shadow.*

BOY: The big thing is a soup ladle.

ANDREA: Ah! A ladle! You see, I would have taken it for a broomstick, but I haven't looked into the matter as you have. Here is your sling.

ANDREA *goes, reading a book.*

BOY (*shouting after* ANDREA): She *is* a witch! She *is* a witch!

ANDREA: You saw with your own eyes: think it over!

The BOY *joins the other boys again. They sing:*

> One, two, three, four, five, six,
> Old Martina is a witch.
> At night, on a broomstick she sits
> And on the church steeple she spits.

Answer **two** of the following questions. Each question is worth 15 marks.

1. In your opinion what is the main idea or message in this extract?
    Base your answer on evidence from the text.

2. Answer either (i) OR (ii)
    (i) What does the children's song/chant tell us about the children?

                                    OR

    (ii) What impression do you get of Andrea from the extract?
         Support your answer with reference to the text.

3. If you were directing this play what would you want the stage to look like? Base your
    answer on evidence from the extract.

QUESTION TWO   (30)

Answer **EITHER 1 OR 2.**

N.B. You must give the name of the play that you choose. You may **NOT** choose either of
the scenes quoted on this examination paper as the basis for your answer.

1. Name a play you have studied and state what you think is its main idea and/or
    message. Explain how this main idea and/or message is communicated in the play.

                                    OR

2. You have been asked to recommend a play for students studying for the Junior
    Certificate.
    Would you recommend the play you have studied for this examination? Give
    reasons based on close reference to your chosen text.

SECTION 2:   POETRY   [30]

The Boy Who Nearly Won the TEXACO Art Competition

he took a large sheet
of white paper and on this
he made the world an african world
of flat topped trees and dried grasses
and he painted an elephant in the middle
and a lion with a big mane and several giraffes
stood over the elephant and some small animals to fill
in the gaps he worked all day had a bath this was saturday

on sunday he put six jackals
in the world and a great big snake
and buzzards in the sky and tickbirds
on the elephants back he drew down blue
from the sky to make a river and got the elephants
legs all wet and smudged and one of the jackals got drowned
he put red flowers in the front of the picture and daffodils in the bottom corners
and his dog major chewing a bone and mrs murphys two cats tom and jerry
and milo the milkman with a cigarette in the corner of his mouth
and his merville dairy float pulled by his wonder horse trigger
that would walk when he said click click and the holy family
in the top right hand corner with the donkey and cow
and sheep and baby jesus and got the 40A bus
on monday morning in to abbey street to hand
it in and the man on the door said
thats a sure winner

Joe Kane

Answer QUESTION ONE and QUESTION TWO

Answer any TWO of the following questions. Each question is worth 15 marks.

1. What are your impressions of the boy in this poem? Support your answer with reference to the poem.
2. This poem has been described as "the whoosh of the imagination at work". Do you agree?
    Base your answer on evidence from the poem.
3. Choose any two features of this poem which really appeal to you. Explain your choice.

Answer **EITHER 1 OR 2** which follow.

N.B. In answering you may **NOT** use the poem given on this paper. You must give the title of the poem you choose and the name of the poet.

1. Choose any poem you have studied which is "wonder-filled" or captures the "whoosh of the imagination".
    (i)   Describe what happens in this poem. (15)
    (ii) How does the poet fill the poem with wonder or show the imagination at work? (15)

                                OR

2. Choose a poem that you think has an interesting title.
    (i)   Considering the poem as a whole explain how the title is interesting. (15)
    (ii) Name **two** other features of your chosen poem which appeal to you and explain why they appeal to you. (15)

SECTION 3:   FICTION   [60]

The following letter is taken from the novel *Remembrance* by Theresa Breslin. Francis, a
soldier, is writing to his friend Maggie. In this letter he shares with her his experiences of
the trenches of World War 1.

My dear Maggie,

*We came up from our rest billet the other night to relieve the troops in the front lines. I
swear the times of our movements must be known to our enemies for they shelled the road
as soon as we began, and stopped immediately we reached the communications trenches. We
left the road at once and crawled through an orchard and some pigpens to reach our
destination by another route. It seems incredible, but among this devastation the trees here
are beginning to bud – after a bitter Winter, Spring now struggles to break through. As the
thaw sets in it is the most punishing work to keep the trenches free of water. The pumps are
poor excuses, and barely work. Our engineers have designed crude constructions which they
call "duckboards" – long square poles of wood with thick crossbars set at intervals. These are
made from whatever can be requisitioned, stolen or scavenged. Wood from shelled and
bombed buildings, empty ration crates, wattle fencing, anything and everything is used.*

*My "hotel" view at the moment is out across the stretch of earth they call No Man's Land
and the very phrase sums up the waste of war – there is a solitary tree stripped of life and
colour, spent ammunition, shrapnel and shell and . . . the unburied dead.*

*I am strangely unafraid of death; there is a trance-like quality to life under these
circumstances. What frightens me more is the death of spirit, that I have so quickly become
accustomed to the sights and sounds of war . . . such an ache in my head and in my heart.*

Francis

Answer QUESTION ONE **and** QUESTION TWO

QUESTION ONE   (30)

Answer **two** of the following questions. Each question is worth 15 marks.

1. What picture of Francis do you get from reading this letter? Explain your answer with reference to the letter.

2.   How does the above letter capture the mood of war?

3. Do you think that the author's use of letter correspondence in this novel is an effective way of involving the reader in the story? Base your answer on your reading of the extract.

QUESTION TWO   (30)

Answer **EITHER 1 OR 2** which follow.

1. Select a novel or short story you have studied which you would recommend to your own age group and explain why you would recommend it.

OR

2. From a novel or short story you have read describe a character that impressed you, and explain why this character did so.

ACKNOWLEDGMENTS 2007 EXAMINATIONS

For permission to reproduce copyright material in these examination papers, the publishers gratefully acknowledge:

'The Boy Who Nearly Won the TEXACO Art Competition' by Joe Kane reproduced by kind permission of the author and New Island Books; extract from *Remembrance* by Theresa Breslin, published by Doubleday and reprinted by kind permission of The Random House Group Ltd; extract from *Mad, Bad and Dangerous* by Christopher Frayling, reprinted by permission of PFD on behalf of Christopher Frayling, © Christopher Frayling 2005; extract from *Galileo* by Bertolt Brecht, Methuen Drama, an imprint of A & C Black Publishers; Martyn Turner for cartoon in the Media Studies Section.

The publishers have made every effort to trace all copyright holders, but if they have inadvertently overlooked any they will be pleased to make the necessary arrangement at the first opportunity.